# Object Technology

## The New Approach to Application Development

**Jerry Cashin**

**toExcel**

New York  San Jose  Lincoln  Shanghai

# Object Technology
## The New Approach to Application Development




This edition published by toExcel Press,
an imprint of iUniverse.com, Inc.

For information address:
iUniverse.com, Inc.
620 North 48th Street
Suite 201
Lincoln, NE 68504-3467
www.iuniverse.com

ISBN:1-58348-565-1

# OBJECT TECHNOLOGY: THE NEW APPROACH TO APPLICATION DEVELOPMENT

## TABLE OF CONTENTS

## LIST OF FIGURES

# LIST OF TABLES

# Introduction

One of the basic premises of object technology is to ensure software engineering behavior mimics that of hardware engineering (or any other kind of engineering for that matter). Components, objects or modules can be joined together from an available repository to form a coherent whole.

Object technology encompasses additional aspects, but software codification and subsequent reuse is vital to the effort. With hardware engineering, attaining the synergy and harmony necessary to create a functioning whole is a task for system integration personnel. Achieving that same functionality using objects remains one of the core challenges for its implementors to manage.

Early euphoria has led to some backlash against the promises of object technology. Initial pioneers touted its improvements over older procedural methods such as greater developer productivity, fewer staff and more effort, reduced computer resource requirements, and a better brand of software.

Unfortunately, it eventually became apparent there were hurdles to overcome to attain these benefits. For example, the technology is complex and difficult to master. In addition, building and maintaining the object repository, the storage medium for software modules, is an innately arduous and labor-intensive task. Additionally, there are the cultural obstacles within each organization that must be overcome before success is possible. Therefore, a sense of disillusionment eventually settled, as objects, much like so many innovations before it, was discovered not to be the sought after miracle solution.

The "reality phase" of object technology adoption is here. Designers, developers, and users now realize objects do represent a major technological advance, but still, there must be a difficult, sometimes traumatic change to the corporate psyche before these benefits can be realized.

By the turn of the century, however, more than 90% of technology managers expect to be using object technology in some form. This usage will either be through their own internally developed module or through the use of object-oriented (OO) development tools or perhaps it will incorporate both methods.

The rationale for object technology is based on issues that directly affect business operations today. These issues include the need for cost reduction, better quality, faster time to market, and closer liaison with customers. Object technology's attributes of inheritance, polymorphism, encapsulation, software reuse, and productivity gains contribute enormously to the satisfaction of these needs.

However, problems must be addressed and overcome. One of these problems is the scarcity of class libraries available to developers. Although class libraries are available at the detail level (for example, to build graphical user interfaces [GUIs]), a shortage exists at the macro level.

Macro-level class libraries manage larger issues such as an accounts payable function. Attaining access to this type of functionality provides developers with a rich resource. Although numerous business object classes are currently under development, it is unclear how they will apply across a wide variety of applications.

Standards are another problem. There are a number of specifications vying for public approval, including common object request broker architecture (CORBA), distributed system object model (DSOM), OpenDoc, common object model (COM), and object linking and embedding (OLE). Several will prosper; some will disappear.

Training is an important aspect concerning objects. The acknowledged difficulty of indoctrinating software developers in the intricacies of object technology is a major concern.

Despite the difficulties posed by objects, their increased use is inevitable. The technology is advancing at a rapid pace on the system software level and increasingly at the user level.

To enable computer professionals to assess the primary issues associated with objects, the report includes chapters on:

1.  Executive Summary

2.  Core Components

3.  Business Benefits of Object-Oriented Technology

4.  Object-Oriented Database Management Systems

5.  Object-Oriented Programming Options

6.  User Interaction

7.  Object-Oriented Applications and Tools

8.  Object-Oriented Analysis and Design

9.  Standards

10. Performance Issues

11. Object-Oriented Implementation Plan

12. Future Trends

Chapter 1, the Executive Summary, provides an overall review of object technology issues. Various methodologies and considerations are analyzed, in addition to supporting technologies that enable developers to build OO solutions for the enterprise.

There are several core components associated with object technology. Chapter 2, Core Components, evaluates these attributes that differentiate objects from older techniques.

Whatever the theoretical and technological benefits bestowed by objects, there must be a measurable advantage to the enterprise before it will be supported. Chapter 3, Business Benefits of Object-Oriented Technology, reviews issues such as software reuse and related productivity gains in order to assess their impact.

There are an endless array of application types, but almost all manage data in one form or another. Chapter 4, Object-Oriented Database Management Systems, examines the myriad of considerations associated with object-oriented database management systems (OODBMS), both from a business and technical viewpoint.

There is no doubt that Smalltalk and C++ have been the primary vehicles for object-oriented programming (OOP). Java is a more recent candidate, although it may be restricted to niche status. Chapter 5, Object-Oriented Programming Options, evaluates programming options, including trends in standardization.

Chapter 6, User Interaction, outlines issues involved with the user interface in an OO environment. Graphical interfaces, programming tools, and developing trends in this area are analyzed.

The state of object technology does not exist solely in the abstract, although it is an important characteristic of objects. There must be applications and tools that help to create them. Chapter 7, Object-Oriented Applications and Tools, reviews the benefits and functions performed by such applications.

Unlike procedural methodology, analysis and design is the most important stage of the development process, even more important than the coding itself. Chapter 8, Object-Oriented Analysis and Design, presents the issues and techniques involved with OO analysis and design.

The role of standards in object technology is significant. There are pseudo official standards, in addition to those that have emerged from the marketplace. The manner in which these competing entities evolve will have a large impact on the technology. Chapter 9, Standards, examines the various choices available.

Chapter 10, Performance Issues, evaluates the issues associated with OO performance, including the influential design variables. Database factors affecting performance are also discussed.

An organization can plan, design, and train personnel, but a system must eventually be implemented. Chapter 11, Object-Oriented Implementation Plan, reviews general implementation principles and examines a client/server (C/S) application based on object technology for further insights.

In an emerging movement such as object technology, future trends constitute a substantial impact upon the issue. Chapter 12, Future Trends, analyzes various tendencies in tools, standards, and products, including the major migration to distributed objects.

# Chapter 1

# Executive Summary

## Object Technology Rationale

The problem with software development at this juncture in the technological journey is its failure to evolve in a manner similar to hardware development. Software lags behind hardware by at least two or three generations and the gap continues to widen even further.

It is generally agreed that conventional software tools and procedures do not adhere to the needs of contemporary system developers. Software systems have become large and complex, difficult to conceptualize, design, implement, and manage. This complexity is expanding rapidly. Architectures and data models now emerging demand vastly improved methodologies to maintain some degree of parity with hardware breakthroughs.

There is, unfortunately, no single solution to resolve this software quandary. Object technology, however, does offer the promise of improving application development and tempering some of the nagging complexity that accompanies so many of today's system development projects.

It can be argued, of course, that object technology is itself a complex mechanism. This is certainly true. However, as additional object tools are developed, there will be some mitigation of this complexity, at least to the end-user. Software developers will also gain relief as some of the more mundane features are automated.

Currently, the majority of software development continues to be practiced in "the old fashioned way," constructed module-by-module, subroutine-by-subroutine, procedurally-based, and serially designed. Software creators are virtually craftsman as opposed to engineers. They manage amorphous guidelines, not a rigorous engineering discipline. Object orientation can help consolidate some of these software development problems.

In the world of object technology, objects and classes are the building blocks of software development. They fulfill a role similar to the electronic components which comprise a hardware device, each component engineered to perform an independent function.

Objects are self-contained entities comprised of both data and procedures. Procedures interact with that data present within the object. Objects that exist for a similar purpose are grouped together in a class. New classes can be created that inherit data and procedures from classes previously developed, which enables the developer to reuse existing classes by simply programming any differences that might be needed during reuse. Objects can transmit messages between them to activate object activity.

Escalating further, libraries of classes can be built for ease-of-access. When such class libraries are specific to a particular function or application, they are often referred to as frameworks.

Formal definitions for related terms include:

- *Objects* – An object is the basic element in OO programming and design. Encapsulated within an object is data appropriate for the object and procedures or methods which interact with that data. In a payroll system, for example, objects such as employees, salaries, and related personnel data, might exist, depending on the design methodology determined by the implementors.

- *Method* – This is the procedure or function that initiates a response when an object receives an incoming message. The nature of the method determines the object's response to such messages.

- *Message* – Interaction among objects is enabled by a message. The object's methodology then manages the specific response to a message.

- *Class* – This represents the aggregation of a set of harmonious objects that share common attributes and methods.

- *Encapsulation* – This first major property of objects bundles methods and variables within an object or class so access is allowed only through the object's own methods, thus producing an integral entity.

- *Inheritance* – This second object property allows objects and classes to share characteristics in a hierarchy of relationships. In a class of Windows, for example, subclasses might focus on error Windows or tutorial Windows. The superclass Windows might have its border and background colors "inherited" through successive subclasses, thus circumventing the need to continuously redefine unchanging attributes.

- *Polymorphism* – This is a third major property of objects. Its capability allows different objects to interpret the same message in accordance with the nature of the object receiving it. A Print message, for example, will be handled differently by an object featuring all text versus one containing graphical data, despite the fact that each is receiving the same message.

Object technology is not a new concept. In fact, object technology represents the imposition of the scientific (or at least engineering) method to the software development process in a general sense. Its formal stirrings, as applied specifically to software, emerged in the late 1960s in Norway. Two workers at Norway's Computer Center, Nygaard and Dahl, created a new language called Simula67. Within this language, they introduced concepts such as classes and subclasses now found in contemporary OO languages.

About five years later, Xerox's legendary Palo Alto Research Center (PARC) became involved in this technology. The Xerox facility, the birthplace of technological innovations such as the Windows phenomenon, developed Smalltalk. Smalltalk was the first full-featured OO language and is perhaps the purest of the OO languages, as every aspect of its design follows the principles of object technology.

Simula67 initially demonstrated the advantages of a class-based language and the concept of storing data and related procedures as a single entity. This latter step saves time and labor by allowing for preprogramming of the common properties of objects.

Simula67 and Smalltalk were virtually restricted to academic circles until the 1980s, when Smalltalk began to gain attention on a limited scale. In the mid-1980s, the pre-existing C language was extended by B. Stroustrup of Bell Laboratories to produce C++. This embellishment to C supports OO programming.

The development of C++ served as the primary vehicle for launching object technology usage in the commercial arena. AT&T and other vendors delivered versions of the language, each with their own extensions and value-added features that immediately rendered each version non-standard. This practice is routine in the computer technology business. As a result of this common practice, attempts are made to write a core standard for the technology that at one point had consisted of a single version.

Object technology has been gaining adherents throughout the 1990s, but its inherent complexity (especially to the software developer who has spent considerable time in the procedural programming world) has mitigated its growth. Complexity, however, also exists in the applications being built. Objects can help in this regard. Once the initial learning curve has been overcome, object technology can meet most of the challenges posed by contemporary system design.

No longer restricted to languages such as C++ and Smalltalk, object technology is now being used in databases, operating systems, user interfaces, and other components of the software development world. Object technology does not offer a panacea for every problem in computer technology, but it does address the issues of application complexity and spiraling development costs more thoroughly than companion technologies.

Many of the elements needed to fully launch object technology into the mainstream are being built. Tools to facilitate application analysis, design, programming, testing, and control are continually refined. In some cases, they are being created for the first time.

Figure 1.1 depicts examples of timelines for implementation of various object technology aids. Note that all of these vehicles are on a sliding curve which indicates they will experience many iterations in the coming years.

## Figure 1.1 Object Technology Introduction

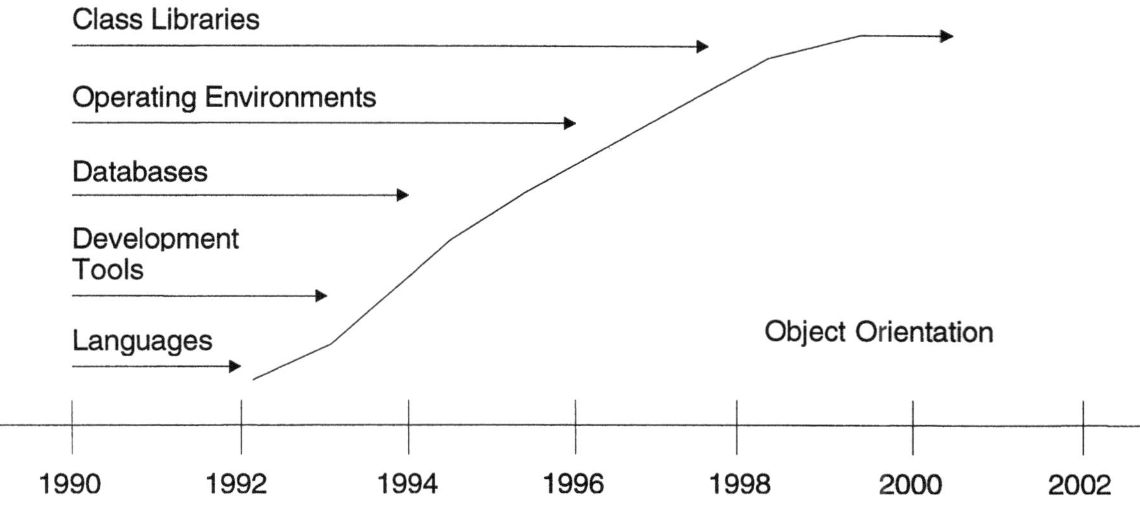


Various studies have been undertaken to measure the productivity gains (if any) that can be anticipated from OO programming. Most have displayed favorable results, although the integrity of their figures is not always entirely accurate. One group reported a 15:1 productivity gain, mostly due to reusability. Another described a 2:1 ratio.

Most of these studies are preliminary and lack the rigor necessary to prompt adequate attention. In some instances, productivity improvements may have been as much the result of upgraded development tools as anything else. However, it is apparent software reuse and object modularity have an enormous impact on the quality of the finished system.

Simply choosing an OO approach does not alone guarantee a first-rate system. C++, for example, is an extremely complex vehicle. Poor programs can be written, just as with any other language. It is vital, therefore, to maintain a set of programming conventions, to follow standards where available, and to continually monitor the quality of the final product. There is no question OO programs are easier to maintain due to their properties of polymorphism, inheritance, and encapsulation.

In the book entitled *Object-Oriented Analysis and Design*, by Martin and Odell, numerous positive attributes associated with object technology are identified, including:

- Reusability

- Faster design

- High quality design

- Stability

- Improved maintenance

- Realistic modeling

- Design independence

- External class libraries

- Reliability

This does not comprise the full list, however. The authors are enamored with object technology. Certainly, the most important of these attributes are software reuse and higher quality systems.

If systems can largely be built with existing objects, projects can be completed in a shorter duration of time. This allows the work to be performed with fewer modifications and to be delivered to the user in an expeditious manner. Quality is also enhanced as fewer changes are introduced during development and existing objects have already been tempered by previous use.

In summary, object technology is a crucial component in the future of software development. Although not an immature technology, much progress is needed in the areas of development tools, databases, and operating platforms. Industry players are moving quickly to respond to this broad array of needs.

## Core Components

The first-time reader of OO precepts often encounters difficulty in assimilating the various nuances associated with this technology, whose concepts and mechanisms are outlined in Figure 1.2.

**Figure 1.2 Object Technology Components**

| Polymorphism | Abstraction |
|---|---|
| Encapsulation | Persistence |

**Key Concepts**

| Object | Message and Method | Class and Instance | Inheritance |
|---|---|---|---|

**Basic Mechanisms**

Another way of looking at objects, for example, is to describe them as any software entity that can support the concept of a name. Another definition centers on the need for procedures (or methods) to be allied with a block of data. The procedure and associated data together comprise an object.

Software objects can range in representation from small to large. This range is comparable to the range of a single grain of sand, for example, to the entire globe itself. The grain of sand may be relatively simple in nature, but represents an integral object within the grander scheme. The globe, on the other hand, is massive and complex. Yet, it is no more or less an object than the grain of sand.

Objects are arranged in a hierarchical manner based upon classes. The class automobile, for example, might include sedans, station wagons, and utility vehicles. These are the various types of automobiles. Each type could have additional subclasses such as manual transmission, automatic transmission, two-door, four-door, and similar differentiations.

Inheritance is another key concept with OO systems. It provides the ability to replicate attributes in one object to other objects without repeatedly reconstituting the duplicate attributes. A programmer simply inherits the attributes and allows for any modifications that must be introduced to the new object.

In the automobile case, for example, the "two-door" object is identical to object "automobile" except it has only two doors. All other characteristics are the same. A developer, therefore, can initiate the inheritance by one object of all the attributes of another without duplicating all of the code in each object. The strength of a feature such as inheritance is its ability to reduce errors and improve operational performance.

Polymorphism allows a command to be transmitted to an object in the form of a generalized instruction, rather than one specific to the recipient. A command such as SEND, for example, could be sent to various objects. They would then interpret that command in the context of their own being. For example, one object may send a text message, another a graphic image, and another may generate an audio response. Each object interprets universally constructed instructions in their own unique manner.

Encapsulation is the technique that protects the integrity of an object, as a casing protects a physical entity. The methods and data bundled together within an object are impregnable to external access methods. No other section of an OO program can directly access the object's data. Only the object's own methods can do so. Communications among objects are possible via messages, but messages cannot access an object's data resource alone. It can "knock on the door, but it cannot go in."

Persistence is another term often associated with object technology. It refers to those selected objects that have a continuing existence at the conclusion of a program's execution. Typically, most objects associated with a program's operation are discarded once the application is terminated. Some, however, are marked for retention. These objects are described as persistent.

## Business Benefits of Object-Oriented Technology

There are numerous benefits to system design, development, and implementation using the OO approach.

Although the development cycle itself is indeed complex, the opposite effect is passed on to the end-user. In an OO user interface, screen images are transmitted to end-users in a manner similar to objects in the real world. This is particularly evident in systems such as Apple's Macintosh (Mac), the Open Software Foundation's (OSF's) Motif offering, and NewWave from Hewlett-Packard (HP). Even Microsoft's Windows demonstrates some OO virtues, although not to the degree found in other products. Computer-aided design (CAD) systems offer another example of component manipulation similar to real world operations.

With the increasing acceptance of OO standards, independently developed general purpose software modules can be combined to achieve a specific organizational purpose. This combination can be performed either on a temporary basis during program execution or set-up permanently for repetitive use. End-users can consider multiple software programs single entities, no matter where they reside or by whom they were developed.

Common functionality in different applications is realized by common shared objects which results in a consistent user interface. This consistent user interface enables developers to focus on application creation matters rather than on application education.

Legacy applications can be protected in the migration to object technology by embedding them in an OO environment. This technique leverages the work already done, while allowing new applications to be built using OO techniques. It may be decided, of course, that one or more of the legacy modules will be a candidate for complete revamping to the object mode. Meanwhile, other older applications will be embedded into newer applications, thus creating a larger, single file "containerized" (with varying levels of integration) within the overall object system.

Reusability of software components is always cited in any OO "benefits list." The achievement of true software reuse produces positive results such as: Diminished costs, enhanced system integrity, and improved operational efficiency. The reused modules have all been previously tested in a working environment. Because the principle of reuse has been employed in the "hardware world" since the beginning of the Industrial Age, no new concepts are being applied. Engineering precepts are finally catching up with software development.

## Object-Oriented Database Management Systems

The basic difference between conventional database management systems (DBMS) and OO versions: OODBMSs store both data and objects. They are encapsulated combinations of data structures along with associated procedures or methods.

Figure 1.3 illustrates the continuous evolution of the various types of database entities that have emerged since the late 1960s. All remain in use, although occasionally in combination with one another. OODBMS products are fewest in number due to their shorter life-span, although their life span will be changing in the future. Figure 1.4 outlines the general structure of an OODBMS.

### Figure 1.3 Database Evolution

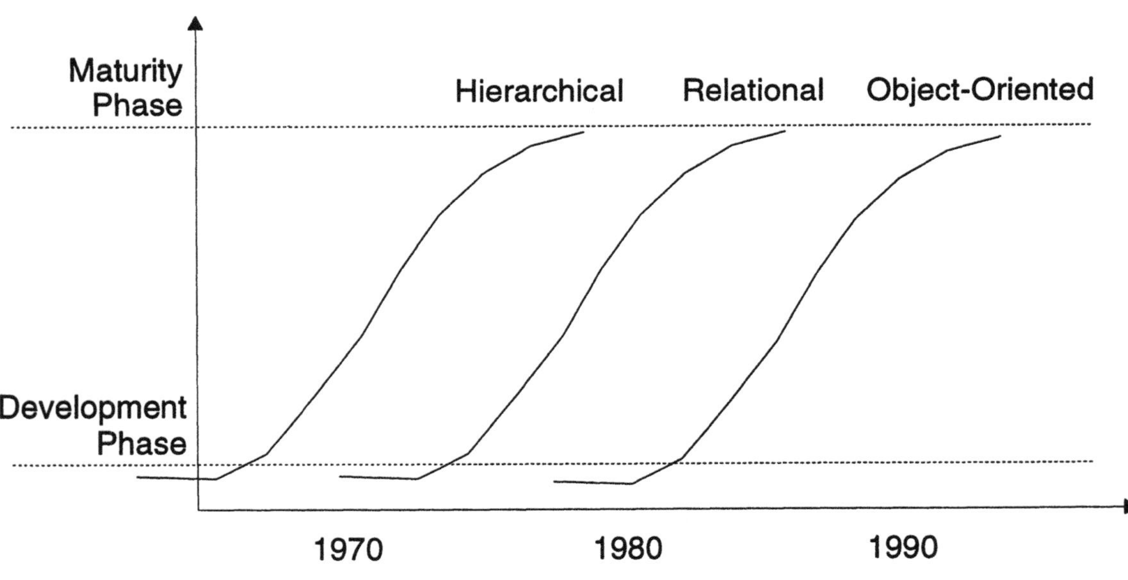

**Figure 1.4 Object Database Management System**

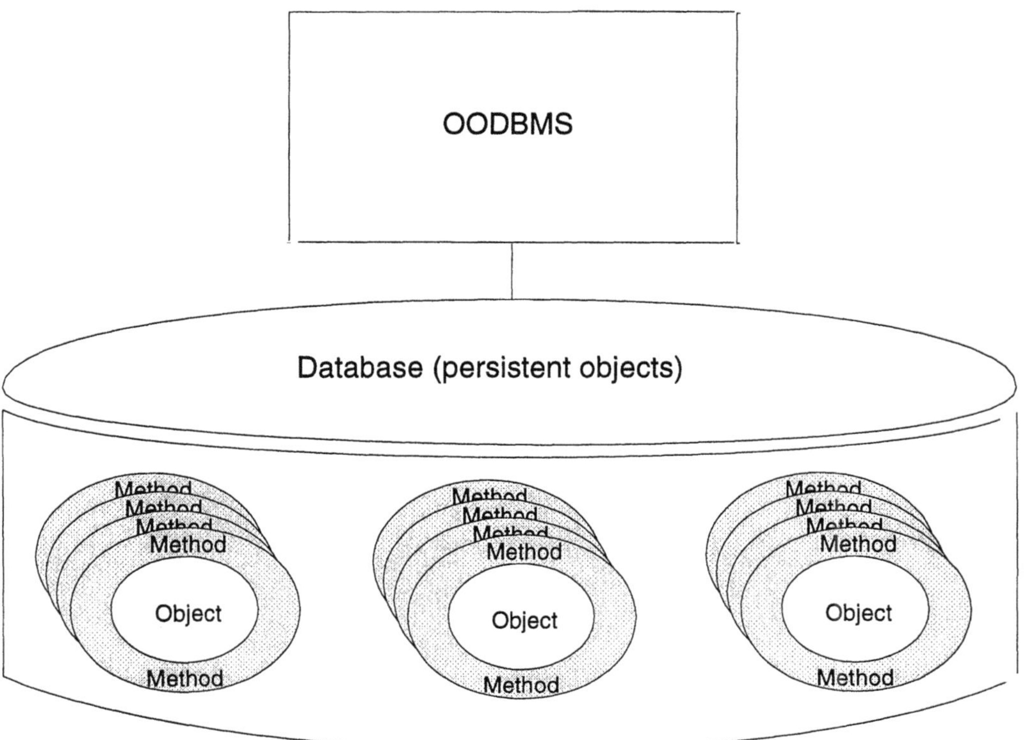


RDBMSs remain the order of the day at present, but an OODBMS offers several differentiations:

- *An OODBMS supports user-defined data structures and operations on them (object classes and methods), rather than limiting users as with a relational model* – The relational model restricts users to instances of a single built-in type such as relations, and a fixed set of operations on them, by means of relational operations.

- *An OODBMS supports the concept of object identity* – The object has an identity independent of its attribute values. This identity can be used to reference the object from within other objects.

- *An OODBMS supports object relationships* – Objects relating to a specific object can be accessed by initiating a method or procedure within that specific object. Thus, related objects do not require a JOIN operation as is used in relational databases. Rather, the related objects are handled as if they were part of the specific object's internal data.

Also, OODBMS offerings typically support concepts such as inheritance and related object sharing mechanisms. A capability to maintain multiple object versions and support for pre-defined object class libraries is usually available.

There are several features found in OODBMS products that have a counterpart in the relational world. For example, there is usually an object class or type definition capability which is similar in intent to a relational data definition language (DDL).

The OODBMS will generally offer an embedded programming language or allow interface to one or more general purpose languages. Some products may provide both capabilities. Among other functions, these languages can build the methods or procedures that form part of an overall object.

Any worthwhile DBMS needs a query language tool to quickly access database contents. Relational databases have the structured query language (SQL) facility, and many object vendors have extended basic SQL to manage objects.

Other components typically accompanying OODBMS products are tools and object class libraries. Tools will perform functions such as database administration and performance monitoring. While object class libraries are primarily used to render database functionality available to accessing programs.

Standards in the specific area of object databases remain rudimentary in nature, although they are rapidly evolving. The Object Database Management Group (ODMG), an industry consortium initiated by companies such as Ontos and Object Design, has been working on a series of OODBMS standards in conjunction with the Object Management Group (OMG).

Some of the areas being worked on by ODMG are a component object model (COM), which is a superset of the OMG model; an object definition language (ODL), which is based on OMG's interface definition language (IDL); and an object query language (OQL), which is based on the relational SQL.

The ODMG has also labored on a C++ language binding and a Smalltalk language binding. These bindings support reading and writing to the same database from either language. ODMG's specification also provides integration capabilities with OMG's common object request broker architecture (CORBA) model.

## Object-Oriented Programming Options

Programming based on traditional procedural methods differs markedly from OO methodologies. In the traditional procedural methods, any procedure can act on any data because the data is a separate physical entity and is subject to alteration by a possibly changing set of procedures.

OO programming, on the other hand, deals with one reality – the object. The object is an amalgamation of data and the procedures (methods) which act upon that data. Objects receive messages and interact with each other through yet additional messages. The property of inheritance also plays an important role by enabling data and methods in an object class to be passed on to its subclass members, in effect recycling validated object components. Figure 1.5 depicts the procedural and object methodologies.

## Figure 1.5 Traditional Method versus Object-Oriented Method

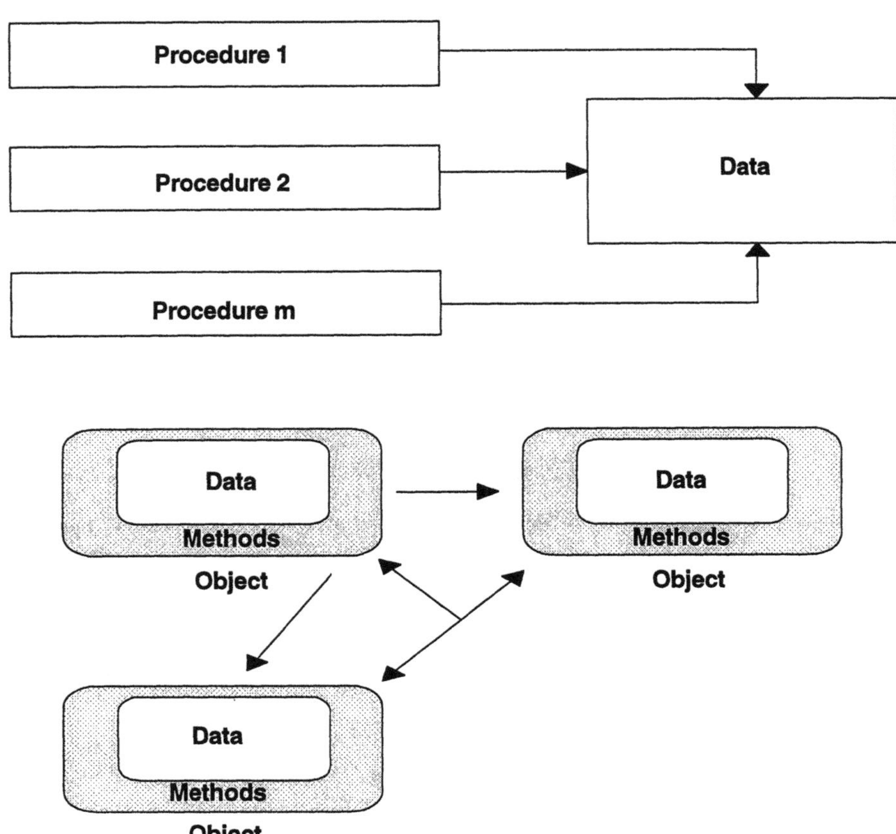


Any programming language, even COBOL, can support object techniques; a task which has been accomplished in some cases. OO extensions have been appended to various languages – particularly C – which was transformed into C++. Whatever the base language, any OO version thereof must support the properties of objects themselves, in addition to inheritance, methods, classes, and messages between objects.

Figure 1.6 depicts the evolution of OO languages from their nascent stirrings – at least in a conceptual sense – in the early 1960s. The language list processor (LISP) introduced the concept of dynamic binding, among other innovations. Simula followed soon thereafter with its inheritance mechanisms and the idea of classes. Modula and Ada introduced the concept of abstract data types in the 1970s. All of these new practices preceded the object model now most commonly linked to the Smalltalk and C++ languages.

## Figure 1.6 Object Language Genealogy

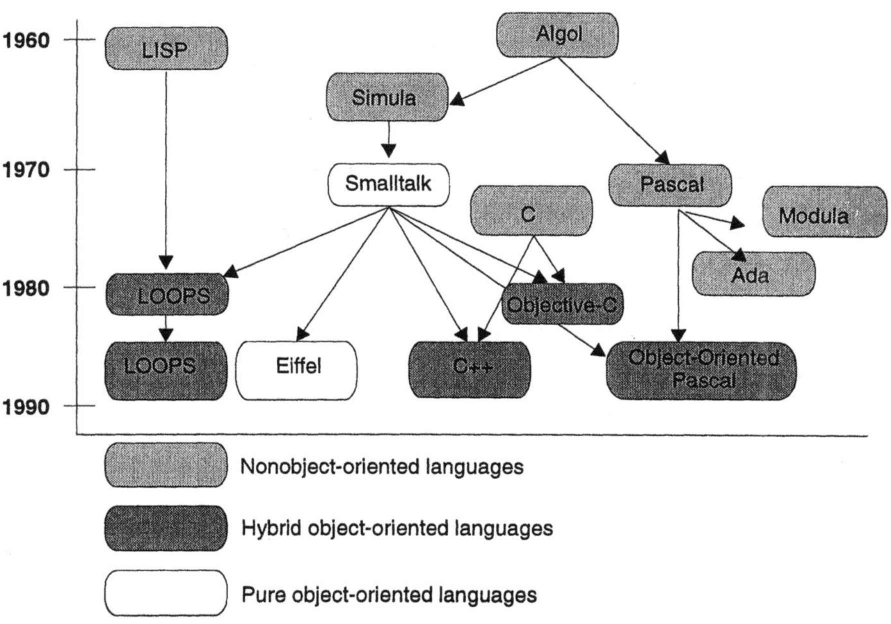


Smalltalk was the initial impetus to a commercially viable OO language. Emanating from the fertile environs of the Xerox PARC, Smalltalk was exposed to numerous interactions during the 1970s and 1980s. This culminated in a company called ParcPlace Systems, which carried the Smalltalk banner into the commercial marketplace.

Until recently, acceptance in that arena has been relatively slow because of several deterrent factors. Procedural languages have been entrenched for decades, millions of lines of code have been produced, and object methods force experienced programmers to leave their "procedural" comfort zone.

The arrival of C++, the OO extended version of C, greatly aided the lethargic migration to object technology. That development and quantum leaps in application complexity has hastened the move to OO languages.

Smalltalk and C++ have emerged as the more important OO languages in the commercial sphere. A "religious" war has been waging concerning their respective merits. Smalltalk is a pure OO language, but does not offer the performance of its rival. C++ is a hybrid product, descended from its ancestral forebear C and comprised of both procedural and object properties, existing as an affront to object purists.

## User Interaction

The modern era in graphical user interfaces (GUI) occurred in the mid-1980s with Apple Computer's launch of its Mac platform. Microsoft's Windows pursued shortly thereafter and it followed, at least conceptually, the direction already established by Apple.

Apple sued Microsoft for intellectual property infringement, but was ultimately unsuccessful in this endeavor. This is perhaps poetic justice because Apple's interface evolved from work done by PARC. Not only did the Xerox PARC provide significant impetus to object technology with their Smalltalk creation, but they were also in the vanguard of early developers of point-and-click interfaces. If the Xerox group had been able to commercially exploit more of their creativity toward their own ends, they would be one of the large software participants today.

Some of the principles first explored at PARC and later implemented in Mac's user interface include:

- The use of an alternative input mechanism to the keyboard – generally a mouse

- Real-time display to the user of ongoing computer activities; this was a novel concept at the time in that it alerts the user as to what is happening in regard to computer activities

- Point-and-shoot capabilities with screen menus appearing or disappearing under user control; the ubiquitous FILE menu in most GUIs illustrates this mechanism

- Heavy use of icons to represent files, software, and system resources; these also are subject to point-and-shoot operations

- A host of other graphic representations, including check boxes, and buttons or analog scales, which enable the user to implement, modify or cancel an action

To the end-user, each of these graphical symbols represents an object in the sense that initiating the symbol activates a chain of actions which involve the use of data and procedures (or methods). To the developer, building user interfaces in an OO system involves linking objects among applications as appropriate to the functionality needed to support a program's execution.

## Object-Oriented Applications and Tools

Since the inception of the computing age, hardware advances have always surpassed software development. Although OO technology represents an advancement in the annals of software capabilities, it still is difficult for developers to maintain the rapid pace of hardware improvements. This has been accurate since the emergence of the first assembly language, throughout the stages of high-level procedural languages, and continuing through the emergence of fourth generation languages (4GLs). It continues to remain true regarding the currently available interactive development vehicles.

There are a variety of descriptors applied to contemporary application development tools. They are referred to as visual programming tools, 4GLs, and GUI builders. In the world of objects, it is highly desirable that a tool follow a model that closely tracks one of the standard models such as that promulgated by the OMG. The tool must support the concepts of objects, classes, methods, and inheritance.

Today's software development environment is generally characterized by the elements shown in Figure 1.7. In effect, developers are entering the heretofore protected sanctuary of system software. Advanced application development demands advanced software techniques.

## Figure 1.7 Software Evolution

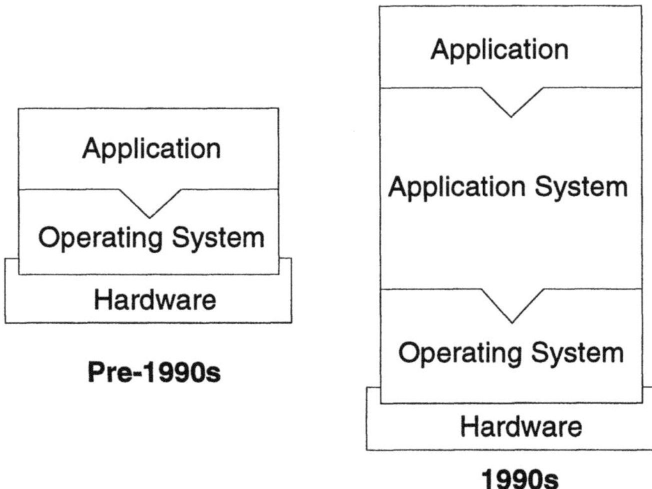



System software builders are simultaneously extending their area of impact into the application arena. This also is motivated by the tremendous complexity of current applications. More must be accomplished on both ends of the spectrum to address today's multifaceted applications.

The pressures of increasing complexity and additional needs of software developers is leading to the configuration depicted in Figure 1.7. It is a new category of system software. This new software mechanism is labeled "Application System" in the figure, but it may also be referred to as other names such as middleware and function layer.

Rather than requiring programmers to embed system-like code into their modules, an Application System provides an integrated set of application and distributed services. OSF's Distributed Computing Environment (DCE) for example, fulfills the requirements needed at this level. Using DCE, a programmer can focus on the needs of the application rather than working on providing distributed services.

The OO language Smalltalk is another candidate for this level of software services. It allows software developers to create applications without necessarily directly linking to the underlying operating system (OS). It also abstracts that OS for application developers – at least partially – and thereby enhances the portability of the created application.

# Distributed Objects

As the name implies, distributed objects refer to the situation whereby software modules reside in different locations, either within the same system or dispersed across a network. The interoperability factor among these object entities is a major component of the technical problem facing software developers.

OO technology is especially useful for managing distributed objects because it facilitates the process of combining mutual incompatible entities in a common protocol. Distributed objects are certainly important in C/S architectures featuring large multiple platform networks.

Technology activists have been working on the problem of distributed objects for several years, particularly in the area of standards. Various standards efforts have emerged in the 1990s, some "official" in nature, others of the de facto variety. All work to provide communication across software modules in different locations. Some current examples include:

- IBM's Distributed System Object Model (DSOM)

- Microsoft's Component Object Model (COM)

- Sun's Distributed Objects Everywhere (DOE)

- HP's Distributed Object Management Facility (DOMF)

- NeXT's Portable Distributed Objects (PDO)

Most of these "standards" are based on OMG's CORBA. They all work reasonably well when constrained within their own domain, but fail dramatically if asked to interoperate. OMG and others, however, are working diligently to remedy the interoperability problem. CORBA 2.x and later versions reflect these improvements.

Distributed objects provide somewhat of a "rough cut" approach to communication among software modules in different locations. To gain more precision, a developer must focus on the use of a single programming language to fine-tune the operation. When doing so, however, interoperability among programs running on different operating systems suffers.

## Object-Oriented Analysis and Design

OO software development offers major benefits by reducing development costs and improving software quality. This intuitive development approach also provides a quicker understanding of software components and enhances project team performance through better communication. Following an established OO methodology provides direction and provides OO developers with a proven, repeatable process for instituting the most effective project management, component reuse, and process improvement technique.

Two OO methodologies, the Shlaer-Mellor methodology and the Rumbaugh Object Modeling Technique (OMT) have emerged as industry leaders, with extensive support from training and consulting organizations, authoritative publications, and software development tools. While there is some overlap between the two approaches, one may offer more benefits depending on the specific type of project being used. The OO methodology checklist in Table 1.1 will help project teams achieve success from objects by selecting the methodology that best meets a project's needs.

### Table 1.1 Object Methodology Checklist

| | Schlaer-Mellor | ✓ | Rumbaugh Object Model Technology | ✓ |
|---|---|---|---|---|
| Proven Successful | Proven on real-time systems development | | Proven on commercial, event-driven systems development | |
| Delivery Objective | Zero defects is most important | | Time-to-market is most important | |
| Emphasis | Rigor, completeness, and correctness in OO analysis; formal process with rules and guidelines | | Readability and expressive power; informal process with recommendations and advice | |
| Iteration and Prototyping | Limits object orientation iteration for efficiency | | Encourages iteration and prototyping | |
| Deliverables | Easily generates formal analysis, design, and implementation deliverables | | Easily generates informal analysis and design deliverables | |
| Design Process | Top-down design | | Middle-out design | |

The first step in selecting a methodology is to define a project's requirements. Table 1.2 compares the requirements of two sample projects.

### Table 1.2 Sample Projects

|  | Project A: Large Satellite System | Project B: CAD Application Package |
|---|---|---|
| Product Characteristics | Real-time, multitasking, multiprocessing; embedded system | GUI, graphics database subsystem; workstation-based |
| Delivery Objective | A complete hardware and software system; zero defects | Release x.x |
| Development Life Cycle | Long development cycle | Iterative development with multiple releases |
| Project Team | Multiple development groups | One project team covers the whole life cycle |
| Deliverables | Formal analysis, design, and implementation deliverables | Informal analysis and design deliverables only |
| Design Process | Top-down design | Middle-out design |

The differences between the two projects – in terms of project focus, size, and duration – are important indicators in matching them to a methodology. Project A, because of these factors, is an example of the type of development for which the Shlaer-Mellor methodology is generally preferred. Project B is an example of the type for which many developers prefer the Rumbaugh OMT. Most Shlaer-Mellor developers complete a rigorous analysis before beginning the transition to design, which reduces defects and provides robust system specifications. Most OMT developers iterate within analysis and design to speed development and facilitate prototyping of key functionality.

Shlaer-Mellor is generally chosen by developers who want a formal development process; Rumbaugh is best suited for those who require more flexibility. However, projects come in all types and sizes, and developers' primary concerns vary. Therefore, the project's specific needs and attributes are paramount in selecting an OO methodology.

The criteria outlined in Table 1.3 can help characterize a development project with respect to the advantages of each of these methodologies.

**Table 1.3 Development Project Characteristics**

| Product Characteristics | 1. What are the key attributes of the application? |
| --- | --- |
| | 2. Is it embedded or host-based? Real-time or event-driven? |
| Delivery objective | 1. Which is more important for the project – zero defects or time to market? |
| | 2. Is a formal process important to the project for ensuring correctness before implementation (such as requirements/analysis/design verification)? |
| | 3. Development cycle – iteration and prototyping. |
| | 4. What is the expected project duration? |
| | 5. Long term or short term? Will development be linear or iterative? |
| Project team | 1. What are the size and characteristics of the development team? |
| | 2. Are there multiple development groups or a single project team? |
| Deliverables | 1. Are there formal or informal analysis and design deliverables? |
| Design Process | 1. Is the project better suited to top-down or middle-out design? |

## Standards

There are numerous standardization efforts underway in the object technology arena. Some such as those promulgated by Microsoft, including OLE, are de facto in nature. Others have broader industry backing such as those put forth by OMG, which consist of more than 400 technology companies interested in OO standards.

The OMG has gained strong momentum over the years as they relentlessly refine CORBA and related standards efforts. The object management architecture (OMA) forms the basis of OMG's architectural framework. Basic capabilities of the OMA are shown in Figure 1.8.

**Figure 1.8 The Object Management Group's
Object Management Architecture**

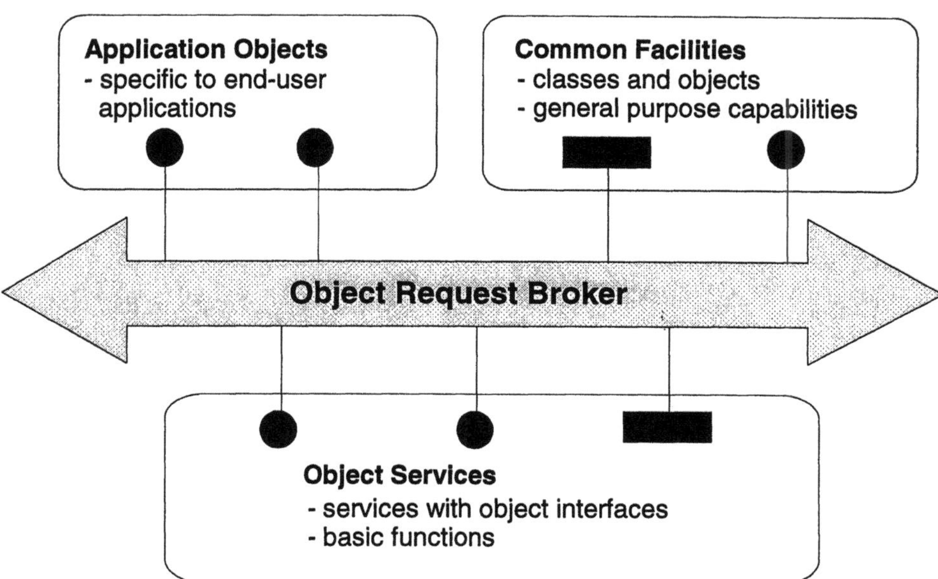


OMA is the center of all the activity undertaken by the OMG. OMG was formed to help reduce complexity, lower costs, and hasten the introduction of new software applications. OMG accomplishes this task through the introduction of the OMA architectural framework along with supporting detailed interface specifications. Implementations are the domain of vendors, end-users, and those developing products and projects to solve a particular computing or business problem. Specifications are the domain of the OMG. These specifications drive the industry toward interoperable, reusable, portable software components based on open, standard OO interfaces.

The OMA Reference Model partitions the OMG mission into practical, high-level architectural components that can be addressed by technology proposers. It forms a conceptual road map for assembling the resultant technologies while allowing for different design solutions (see Figure 1.9).

## Figure 1.9 Object Management Group Reference Model

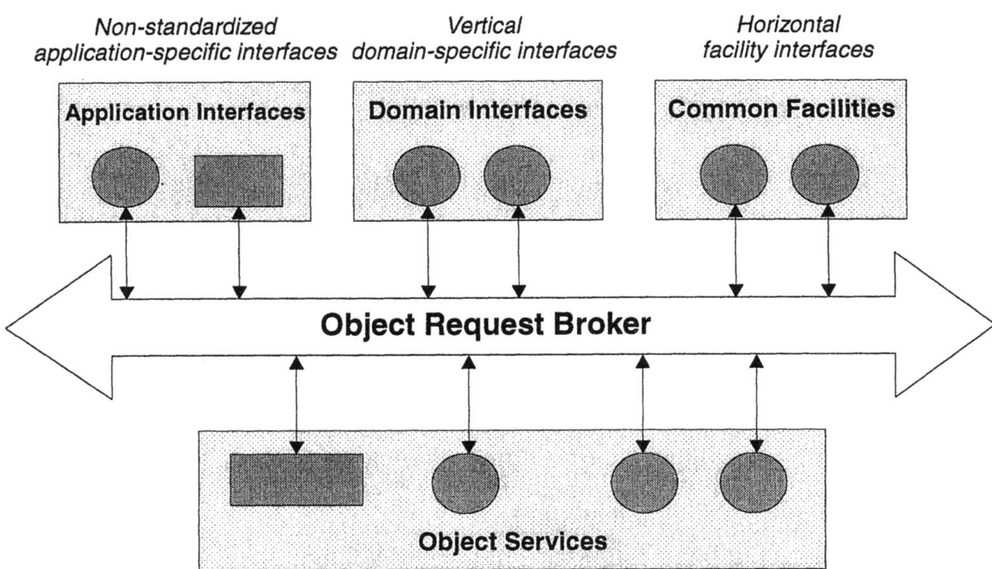


The Reference Model identifies and characterizes the components, interfaces, and protocols that compose the OMA, but does not in itself define them in detail. The OMA can be viewed as three major segments consisting of five critical components:

1. *Application-Oriented* – the OMA characterizes interfaces and common facilities (CFs) as solution-specific components that rest closest to the end-user.

2. *System-Oriented* – Object request brokers (ORBs) and object services are more concerned with the "system" or infrastructure aspects of distributed object computing and management.

3. *Vertical Market-Oriented* – Domain interfaces are vertical application domain-specific interfaces. These, coupled with combinations of inherited CF and OS interfaces, will provide critical application frameworks to a wide variety of industries.

All communications between components are managed by the ORB, the foundation of the OMA. ORB technology is considered to be one of the most important approaches for deploying open, distributed, heterogeneous computing solutions. OMA assumes underlying services provided by a platform's OS and lower-level basic services such as network computing facilities, are available and usable by OMA implementations.

OMA components require clarification to first-time implementors. Some of the major components are:

- *Object Request Broker* – Commercially known as CORBA, the ORB is the communication's heart of the standard. It provides an infrastructure allowing objects to converse, independent of the specific platforms and techniques used to implement the objects. Compliance with the ORB standard improves portability and interoperability of objects over a network of heterogeneous systems.

- *Object Services* – These components standardize the life cycle management of objects. Interfaces are provided to create objects, control access to objects, monitor relocated objects, and to control the relationship between styles of objects (class management). The generic environments in which single objects can perform their tasks are also provided. Object services provide for application consistency and help increase programmer productivity.

- *Common Facilities* – CFs provide a set of generic application functions that can be configured to the specific requirements of a particular configuration. These are facilities that sit closer to the user such as printing, document management, database, and E-mail facilities. Standardization leads to uniformity in generic operations and to better options for end-users to configure their working environments.

- *Domain Interfaces* – Domain interfaces represent vertical areas that provide direct interest functionality to end-users in particular application domains. Domain interfaces may combine some common facilities and object services, but are designed to perform particular tasks for users within a certain vertical market or industry.

- *Application Interfaces* – While not an actual OMG standardization activity, application interfaces are critical when considering a comprehensive system architecture. Application interfaces represent component-based applications performing particular tasks for a user. An application is typically built from a large number of basic objects – some specific to the application at hand, others domain specific, specific from object services or built from a set of common facilities. These applications greatly benefit from the strengths of robust object systems development. Better abstraction of the problem space and solution, reusability of components, and far simpler extension over time are well-known aspects of sound object application development (see Figure 1.10).

## Figure 1.10 Application Frameworks

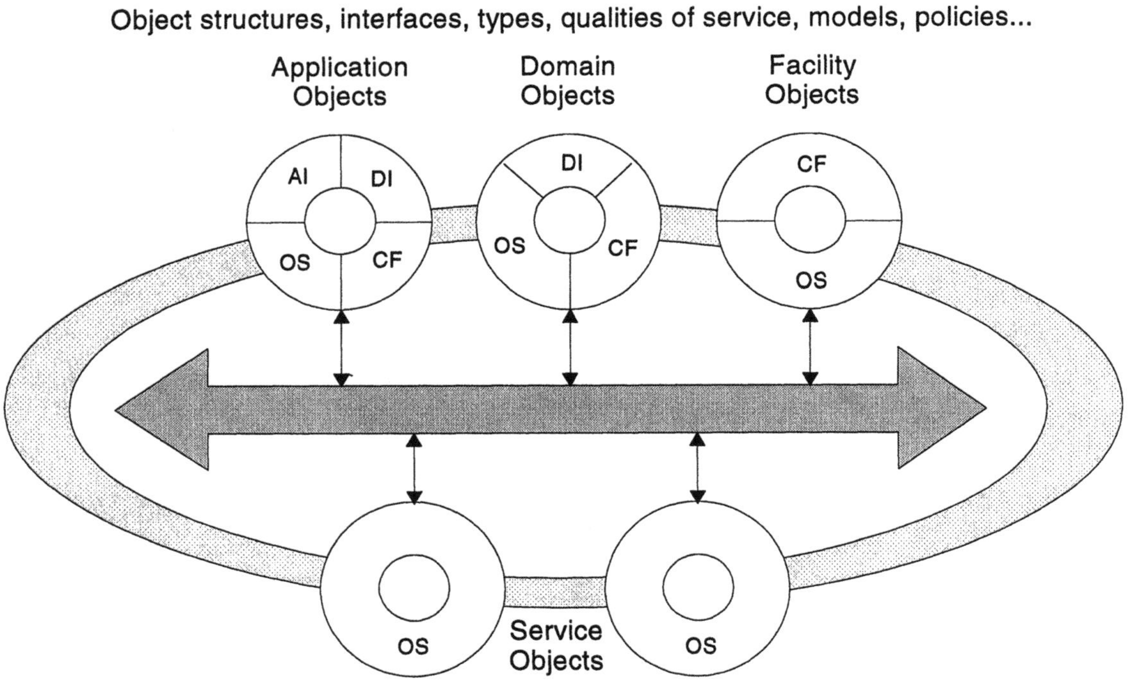

## Performance Issues

Performance in an OO system is affected by many factors, but manipulation of objects themselves – particularly when resident in an OODBMS – is the single most important factor impacting performance. Therefore, it is vital to evaluate the attributes of an OODBMS before acquiring it for operational use. This evaluation is in addition to measurement of other system components such as software, networks, and platforms.

For many commercial, engineering, scientific, and technical applications, high performance in handling complex, non-record-oriented data – such as two dimensional (2-D), three dimensional (3-D), voice, video, graphics, and text — is the single largest factor in the success or failure of an object database system. Specifically, object database systems must attain performance orders of magnitude faster than their relational predecessors to adequately manage this type of data.

To evaluate performance, focus on three things: Benchmarking, tuning options, and overhead issues. Benchmarking is the process of viewing published benchmarks and performing in-house benchmarks. Tuning options are the features an object database system provides to obtain the highest performance from an application. Overhead issues refer to the amount of overhead expenses the object database system adds to an application in terms of network, main memory, and disk requirements.

The type of performance required for each application will vary from application to application. The important metrics for benchmarks are object traversal, object retrieval speed, object creation, and object update.

- *Object Traversal* — How fast can software traverse a group of related objects in memory? This is a crucial measurement for highly visual applications in which a GUI is used to manipulate data.

- *Object Retrieval Speed* — How long does it take to locate a group of objects and make them available to an application?

- *Object Creation* — How long does it take to build a database?

- *Object Update* — How long does it take to update or store a group of objects?

  Many database systems perform satisfactorily out of the box, but are not tunable for more demanding applications. Key features to look for include: Tunable cache, object clustering, lock probes and time-outs, lock caching, data fetching policy, and dynamic indexing.

- *Tunable cache* — This feature provides the ability to adjust cache sizes on client and server machines to optimize the trade-off between reuse of previously accessed objects and efficient use of available memory.

- *Object Clustering* – Clustering is the single most effective tuning facility the object database application designers have at their disposal. Clustered storage optimizes the retrieval of related information by physically storing logically related objects in the same area on disk. Support for object-level clustering affords the programmer the option of placing individual objects next to each other in user-controlled clusters and to control the number of objects allowed in each cluster. This facility incorporates two advantages. First, by co-locating objects that must be retrieved together, users can minimize the disk input/output (I/O) required to access a group of objects. Secondly, these facilities can be used to manage and eliminate unnecessary concurrency conflicts without suffering the performance degradation associated with object-level locking techniques.

- *Lock Probes and Time-outs* – Locking should be completely transparent; an application simply accesses objects. If a lock is held on an object by another transaction, the default action is usually for the application to wait until the lock is available. Lock time-outs and probes enhance the object database system locking model by enabling an application to monitor the availability of a lock without incurring substantial waits or potential deadlock situations.

- *Lock Caching* – The ability of an application on a client workstation to reuse locks from transaction to transaction without communicating with the server is the difference between sub-second and multisecond response for many applications where the user is visiting the same data in consecutive transactions.

- *Data Fetching Policy* – This feature controls the granularity of data transferred from the server to the client at a given time. In circumstances where large amounts of data must be scanned – as in multimedia – specifying the amount of data to be automatically fetched to the client will significantly improve performance.

- *Add and Drop Indexes* – The object database system should be able to dynamically add and drop indexes to control the trade-off between query performance and update performance.

Performance is defined as obtaining the maximum amount of work from a given system or group of systems in a network. Because the object is the building block for all OO applications, a major consideration for using any object database system is the overhead that the database imposes on objects. If the object database system is inefficient in managing individual objects, the resource consumption issues will compound themselves as applications start using thousands and millions of objects. Key questions to identify include:

- *What fixed overhead is carried by each object?* Some object database systems carry more than 50 bytes of data per object because of several layers of indirection required to find objects. All object database systems differ widely in this area.

- *What is the fixed overhead that can be carried by a database?* During an evaluation, verify the minimum size possible for a database and determine the size of the database as more objects are loaded.

- *What is the size of a reference from one object to another?* While all databases must address enormous amounts of data, a reference to another object is 32 bits in some systems, while in others it is as much as 128 bits. In most OO applications, the majority of data consists of references to objects. This overhead is the dominant factor in determining the size of the database.

- *Does the object database system keep separate locks for each object?* Because OO applications are based on objects often composed of smaller objects – perhaps several layers deep – object-level locking can place a significant load on the central processing unit (CPU) and halt applications. These types of applications require higher levels of granularity for locking and transfer of data. Look for a database system that provides the ability to tune the granularity of locks without changing the application.

- *Does the object database system move objects from client to server one at a time?* Because applications will typically involve thousands of objects, moving groups of objects to the client in an efficient manner is a major factor in multiuser environments. Look for a database system that provides the ability to set the granularity of data transfer between a client and server.

## Object-Oriented Implementation Plan

OO technology is based on the premise that, data (an object) is more stable and easier to formalize than functions. Therefore, basing software analysis and development on objects, rather than on functional behavior, leads to more stable designs and more maintainable implementations. Many industry experts have stated that OO technology offers major productivity advantages over traditional software development techniques.

Users, therefore, are adopting object technology in greater numbers each year. It is imperative that these users have an implementation plan. Some of the major issues to consider in this regard are:

- Accurate assessment of project requirements and deliverables

- An effective implementation plan

- Understanding OO concepts and terminology

- Management and staff commitment

- Software reuse at multiple levels of abstraction

- Selection of tools best suited to the project's needs

An accurate assessment of a project, followed by careful and well-ordered planning, is the key to success in this area. Accurate assessment involves not only a clear view of the end product (for example, hardware or software, embedded, real-time or C/S), but also a realistic view of any constraints that may affect the process. Constraints may include regulatory standards, documentation requirements, and formal and informal scheduled design deliverables. Time is a constraint in any project and must be carefully balanced against project needs.

After needs and constraints have been determined, an orderly implementation plan must be established. This plan will vary considerably among projects, but following certain steps provides a useful guideline. These steps include:

- Establish a project team and assign specific roles or tasks. For example, who will be the analysts, designers, architects, programmers, and configuration managers? Responsibilities should be carefully defined to avoid duplication, confusion, and miscommunication.

- Establish a software development process. A well-defined process is one of the most important success factors in OO development.

- Define the required project life cycle (traditional or iterative), deliverables, and milestones

- If appropriate, carefully select a methodology that adheres to the team structure, process, and life cycle, plus all applicable constraints

It is essential to understand a problem before designing its solution. The analysis model represents what is known about the problem, including its scope. Prototypes and other exploratory work augment the analysis model; they cannot replace it. Developers must be careful not to let design and implementation concerns confuse their basic understanding of the problem at hand.

OO methodologies simplify the analysis process by encouraging developers to construct three complementary views of a system:

1. The Data/Object/Entity view describes what data/objects/entities are contained in and managed by the system.

2. The Behavioral/Control view describes the life cycles of an entity or object in terms of an evolving status over time, known as explicit states, and transitions between them.

3. The Functional view describes the data transformations in the system and their data dependencies.

Once the requirements have been established and the problem defined, developers must identify the fastest path from analysis to design. Large and complex problems must be divided into smaller, separate units so they can be worked on in conjunction with one another. Problem domains can be arranged in a hierarchy, in which they support or constrain other domains according to their hierarchical relationships.

The design process maps a problem specification into a set of implementation technologies. In an OO design, at least two views of a system must be considered: Class design, which focuses on inheritance relationships, reference relationships, and dependencies; and method design, which focuses on method interfaces and modularity issues.

There are many OO methodologies, some that are very new and others that are well established. Most support the same basic concepts: Objects and classes; object attributes and methods; encapsulation of data and behavior into objects; object communication using messages; polymorphism as an aspect of object behavior; inheritance and aggregation; and object states. Understanding these concepts is critical to using object technology to implement a system or software solution. Moreover, these concepts are treated somewhat differently by the various methodologies currently available.

The most common pitfall in this area is the tendency to rush into implementing OO concepts without sufficient understanding of how they function. For programmers with many years of experience in traditional methods, approaching design in an OO manner may involve adopting a radically different thought process, and this adjustment takes time. Data abstraction, encapsulation, inheritance, and polymorphism may be new concepts to many practitioners. Newcomers to OO often want to immediately use all of these tools before receiving training and proper grounding. Project leaders and management must take the initiative to establish policies to prevent this mistake, which typically leads to rework and lost time. Education for the team is crucial, as is the availability of an experienced advisor throughout the course of a first project.

Management support is often overlooked by companies adopting OO technology, although it can be critical to the success of a project. Software managers and developers must accept the fact changes in procedures and organizational structure may be necessary. In addition, an object technology perspective must be adopted to ensure the success of an OO development project. Success depends on the willingness of management to commit the necessary time and funds to fully train all personnel who will be involved in the new technology and process. Success also depends on a commitment to identify, evaluate, and acquire the tools best suited to the needs of the team.

The benefits of reusable software components are compelling. They include:

- Less software to build and maintain

- Standard components may be of higher quality than custom-built code

- Systems built from standard components may be easier to understand than systems built from scratch

However, reusable software is difficult to design. One way to begin is to reuse higher-level designs and specifications rather than low-level components. If a subsystem design can be reused, all of its individual components need not be reusable.

For projects that require components to be designed for reuse, developers with experience in this process have offered observations:

- *Focus on classes that correspond to the particular application*

- *Allow the general purpose to evolve from special purpose* – This will result in classes that are needed and will be used, and that reflect real requirements

- *Document all classes* – A class is more likely to be reused when it is documented and when users have confidence that it works properly

- *Avoid building more than a few generic container classes* – If more generic container classes are required later, they can be purchased

- *Purchase GUI libraries rather than spend time building them*

Developers often place tool selection at the top of their list for successful OO development. However, doing so may prove costly. There are many excellent tools available, but most are intended to support a particular method, which is itself intended for a particular type of project. The rush to buy tools without matching them to specific project needs, which could destine a project to failure from the outset.

There are several important points to consider when evaluating tools. Many tools:

- Provide only partial support for a particular methodology

- Do not operate on every hardware platform and under every OS

- Do not handle large problems well

- Do not support multiuser environments

It is essential to thoroughly assess a tool's benefits and its limitations to avoid problems later in the development cycle.

## Object-Oriented Client/Server Systems

C/S computing became widely accepted because of the processing power that emerged on desktops and local area networks (LANs). C/S computing harnesses the power of widely distributed processing by placing portions of applications and data on the proper platform in terms of price/performance and ease-of-use.

That C/S applications inherently reflect the business model to a greater degree results from the end-user orientation of C/S applications and the faster speed at which C/S applications – at least small-scale applications – can be developed. Compared to the host-based applications familiar to users, C/S applications appeared well-suited to their needs.

Object technology brings four advantages to C/S development:

1. *Objects change very little, while processes and procedures constantly change* – As a result, objects are considerably more stable elements with which to build an application. A customer will always posses a name, address, phone number, and other essential information. This information can be captured as an object, encapsulated and stored. Once the customer object has been created, it may be used in a wide number of applications for a variety of business process needs.

2. *Objects reflect the real world* – When designing an application, it is more natural to think in terms of actual business entities – customers, invoices, products – than in procedures and data structures. Using objects, a user can design an application by describing familiar entities: What they do, and what they need to perform their jobs. This is more sensible than trying to design the application in terms of inputs, outputs, and data flows and expecting the finished product to resemble the business. In addition, enacting changes will be much easier. The real world nature of objects enables business people to communicate with corporate developers in a common language of recognizable business objects.

3. *Objects reduce complexity* – Programmers can work with objects without knowing how the object itself works. To use an object in an application, they need only know what it is and what messages the object responds to, not necessarily how it works.

4. *Objects are reusable* – The customer object, for instance, can be used in a billing application, a customer service application, and many others. A transaction object can be used in any application that uses transactions. Through inheritance, new child objects can be quickly created that obtain by succession the functionality and attributes of the parent object. The terms "parent" and "child" are used to describe the relationship between a class and a subclass of objects. As the term implies, parent classes are higher in the hierarchy than child classes. The programmer need only define the new attributes that render the child object different from the parent object. This technique has the potential for delivering substantial increases in programmer productivity, thereby dramatically reducing development time.

For example, when the inheritance mechanism is used to add a new type of bank account, the new account automatically contains the inner workings of an account (for example, deposit, withdrawal, balance). The only necessary development involves determining those attributes that differentiates the accounts. With reuse and inheritance, object technology promises to usher in an era of application development by assembly of encapsulated modules.

Objects present a few of their own problems, many of which are caused by the relative immaturity of supporting technology. Programmers, for example, often experience difficulties when reusing objects because they are not certain as to the precise functions of a stored object. The actual code must be studied, which ultimately defeats the purpose of the exercise.

Another problem with objects is their interoperability – or lack thereof. There are standards efforts underway, and their work has been quite effective. However, product implementation of these standards takes time. Meanwhile, it is difficult to integrate object implementations of different vendors.

To reach the pinnacle of object development, several techniques must evolve, including:

- *OO design* – The ability to build applications by defining objects that represent business entities such as customers, products, and sales and describing the interactions between these objects

- *Readily apparent reusability of objects through meaningful business* – Similar descriptions and definitions and easily grasped roles and interfaces

- *Consistent object definitions and terminology from analysis through design to source code* – For example, where the term "customer" is defined the same way through the entire development cycle

- *Pre-defined object classes for technical and GUI objects* – The encapsulation of groups of low-level objects that collaborate to perform a recognizable high-level function such as data access

- *Tools* – To create and manage class libraries

- *Automatic object generation* – The ability to automatically turn high-level, object-based designs into application code including object definitions, screen definitions, and logic

- *Methodology transparency* – Allowing a developer to choose any design methodology

## Future Trends

There will be numerous future initiatives emerging in object technology in the coming years. Standards, development tools, and object libraries will all become more prominent than they are currently. Much of this work, however, although ultimately important to the end-user, will proceed "behind the scenes."

Developments on other fronts will more directly impact object users. One of the major areas of interest is Microsoft's OLE. Whatever its merits in comparison to DSOM, CORBA, and OpenDoc, OLE is ubiquitous. Its future – and object technology's future in general – will travel a similar, if not identical path.

The OLE product represents one of Microsoft's main weapons for invading the enterprise, including the world of mainframes, tightly managed applications, and secure environments. While Microsoft does indeed control the desktop, it is but a grain of sand in enterprisewide systems. They are working to change this situation, however. Microsoft is licensing OLE source code to other vendors. Software AG, for example, is porting parts of OLE to non-Microsoft platforms, including IBM's enterprise standard – multiple virtual storage (MVS).

In another aggressive move, Microsoft has purchased Netwise, Inc. and its remote procedure call (RPC)-based middleware product inventory. This acquisition will enable them to link LAN configurations to MVS. Again, MVS is the reigning monarch of enterprise computing, containing all the features and options necessary in corporate settings.

Previously, OLE technology had been restricted to Windows. The Mac has also been a viable player, but OLE usage there has been minimal. It has predominantly been a Windows product. This is fine on the desktop, but to become a viable enterprise participant, OLE must interact with the products of big time industry "iron." IBM mainframes will be a very large participant in corporate C/S architectures.

Microsoft's acquisition of Netwise enables it to offer a fuller C/S solution, especially when integrating MVS into the C/S solution. Netwise's middleware product – TransAccess – interconnects LANs, desktop devices, and MVS-based systems including DB2 and customer information control system (CICS).

The TransAccess product supports both SQL access and remote function initiation techniques. Remote function initiation techniques improve distributed access to CICS transactions.

Several spin-offs of the core OLE technology are underway to further enhance Microsoft's enterprise profile. Network OLE provides developers with OO interfaces to distribute computing resources. OLE integration enables developers to create OLE components on network-based servers. OLE DB is an effective means for database access and OLE transactions. Each product is targeted for enterprise support and is in various stages of development.

As is always the case when enterprise computing is the issue, complexity multiplies. Where OLE started as a single entity designed to support a few desktop functions, it must now manage issues far beyond its original scope. Whether it has the necessary robustness to carry added responsibilities must be determined through time.

OLE will be successful in the enterprise, at least to some degree, but what about CORBA, DSOM and OpenDoc? There is a strong probability that they will all prosper. Each approach will have its proponents and areas of strength. After living with numerous choices in the past, the technology world should be quite comfortable managing merely two or three object models.

# Chapter 2

# Core Components

## History of Objects

The historical progression of object technology has, in reality, been regressing. The initial focus was on OO programming languages. Attention was then directed to analysis and design techniques. Attention later shifted to project controls, quality measurements, and development management.

This sequence of events is the exact opposite of most new ventures. As a result, OOP languages are relatively mature, whereas project management, analysis, and design capabilities are lagging. Such a convoluted situation places object development projects in a certain degree of jeopardy.

Objects themselves are virtually void of technology's growing pains because they ultimately model situations in the real world. The rationale for objects: They represent real world functions.

An object has attributes which parallel real world properties. These attributes could, for example, be items such as color, size, and shape. An object also has methods which control the actions of the object.

Numerous objects would exist in a payroll system. Among them would be employees, their relevant data, and their payment history. The employee object attributes would typically consist of name, salary, and deductions. Methods or procedures associated with this object might be actions such as Increase Salary, Transfer, and other issues deemed appropriate to the company's mode of operation.

Locating a particular object in a system once it has been stored is an entirely different anomaly when compared to building an object. There must be some identification technique introduced for such a purpose. This technique is typically accomplished by the object's system environment. Identifications can range from a simple sequential numbering system to virtual memory address.

In most systems, there will be groups of objects that are assembled into classes. They will share attribute and method definitions, but not attribute values. Classes – or groups of objects – are an important concept in object technology. The payroll system would have an employee class and payment history class. The term "class" is sometimes used interchangeably with the term "type."

Within a class of objects, the individual object is referred to as an "instance." In an operational scenario, two functional steps are employed to create or delete objects of a class, generally known as "construct" or "destruct." The awkward phrase "instantiation" is occasionally used to describe object creation.

A distinction is often made between active objects and passive objects. As their names imply, active objects can invoke interactions among themselves, whereas passive objects only react to incoming activity. In the payroll example, an employee promotion would result in change to employee record initiated by one or more active objects. Such changes would not be invoked by an object such as a payment history. Payment history is a passive receptacle for information, but not an initiator of such information.

The act of assigning objects to specific classes is referred to as "classification." An object occasionally is assigned to multiple classes. In other occasions, an object may be moved from one class to another. Various object models approach these functions in a different manner, but the concept itself is important.

An object can manifest different roles in a business process. For example, an accounting object can represent a payment function in purchasing and a collection function in sales.

It can be said, of course, that classes themselves are objects – or perhaps "superobjects." There can also be classes of classes – "metaclasses." The hierarchical spiral can be complex, at least in an intellectual sense. Various object models address these issues in unique ways.

As object technology matures, issues such as superobjects, metaclasses, and possible aggregations that may be concocted will become transparent to the average user. Within the technology itself, subclasses of expertise will arise. Some technologists will specialize in "enterprise-level" objects. Others will labor in the specialty of low-level, individual-type classes or objects. Tools and middleware that shield most users from the vagaries of object creation and manipulation will be developed.

## Summary

An object is defined by its class. Objects are individual instances of a class. For example, an object called "Fido" can be created from class "Dog." The Dog class defines what constitutes a Dog object. All OO languages have a capability to create object instances from a class definition.

Additional objects of the class Dog might be labeled Rover or Hunter, for example. This same class named Dog can delineate the messages with which the multiple Dog objects interact. Examples of such messages might be RUN, STAY, and similar messages appropriate to the overall class and individual objects.

A method is an action that conveys the intent of the message within the context of the object where the message resides. The code executes from within an object.

## Classes

To create an object from a class as depicted in Figure 2.1, the developer creates an instance of that class – an object. The definitions used by the class are employed to create an individual object that has characteristics from the class.

# Figure 2.1 Classes of Objects

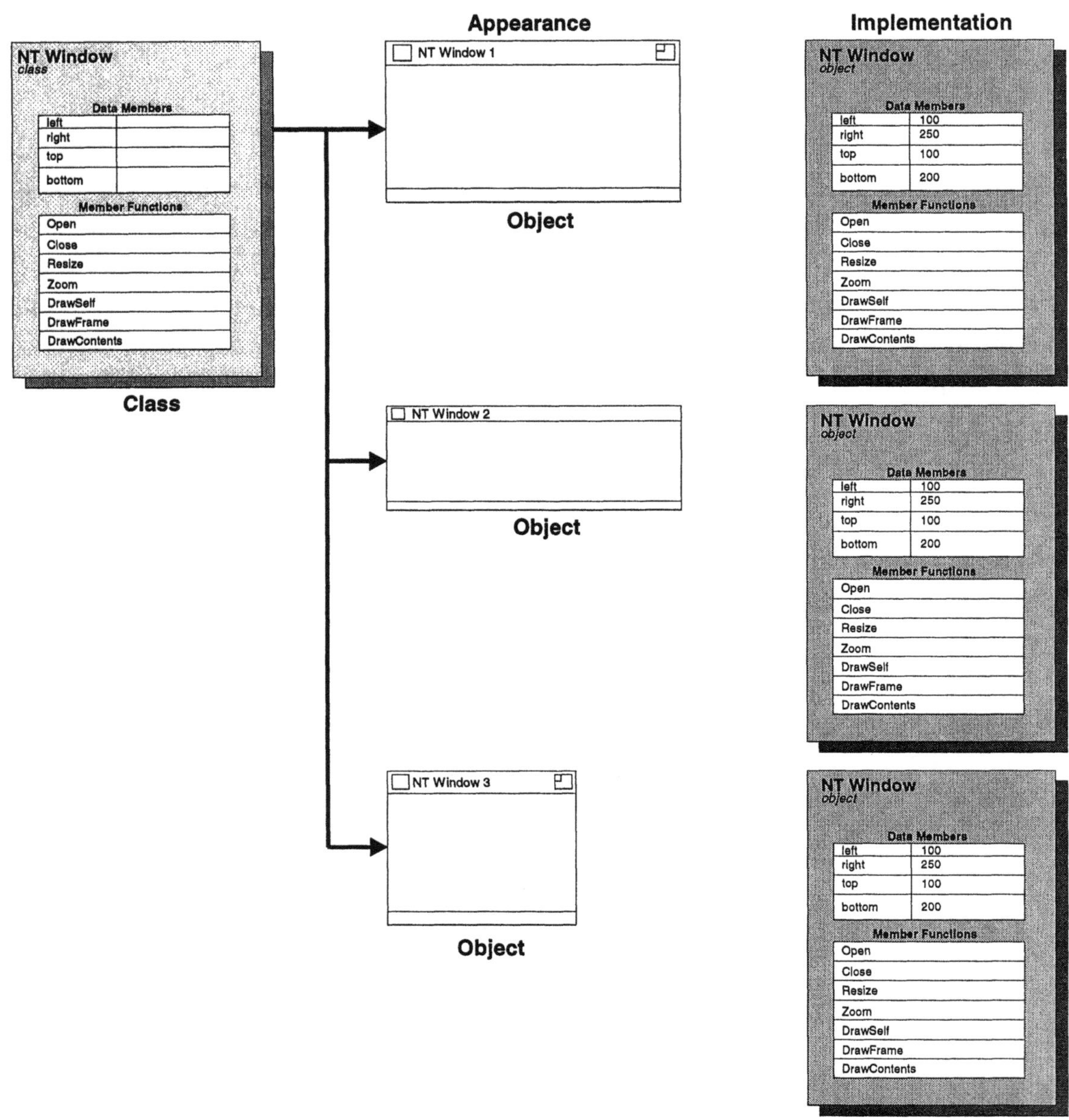


Creating an instance, also known as instantiation, saves the work of regenerating data members and member functions each time the program creates an object. The process builds a new object ready to use by implementing a single line of code.

Every instantiation creates a new set of data, but shares the code that implements object functionality. Each object in Figure 2.1 has the same data categories as all other objects shown, but actual values will differ depending on the specific tasks intended for the various objects.

There are some software vendors who claim they utilize objects, but in fact provide libraries of object classes. Direct classes can invoke instantiation to create actual "working objects." Because of object technology's attribute of inheritance, complete regeneration of previously developed routines is unnecessary.

Many commercial products support class libraries that can be used and reused through instantiation and generation of subclasses. A "class hierarchy" describes the trail of inheritance with a family of related objects. Following instantiation of an object, its inherited properties are determined by its place in the class hierarchy. It can also be part of a "containment hierarchy," whereby an object can contain and be contained by other objects.

Class library benefits include several attributes:

- *Objects and their related classes* – Enable large, complex problems to be divided into smaller, more manageable tasks

- *Encapsulation* – Protects the integrity of an object's data, yet permits interaction with other objects

- *Inheritance and subclassing* – Supports the derivation of new objects from existing classes, thus diminishing the need to "reinvent the wheel" when creating new functions

- *Class hierarchies and containment hierarchies* – Offer an efficient method for modeling real-world objects and their relationships

Subclasses are occasionally referred to as "derived classes." "Superclasses" are even higher in the hierarchy than parent classes.

In terms of actual development work, a programmer typically begins with a pre-existing class library which contains useful, utilitarian programming modules. A programmer would then customize this general purpose class library by creating new subclasses for the application as needed.

The subsequent application-specific class library, most of which has generally been inherited from the original class library, is referred to as a "framework." A framework, therefore, is a class library modified to meet the requirements of a new functional task. Because all frameworks are specific to an application's unique needs, they are not as useful for other developments as generic class libraries.

## Inheritance

Inheritance is a vital component of object technology. A developer can take one class and create a subclass (or derived class in C++ terminology) from the original class. This new subclass inherits all the attributes of that original class. In fact, it now constitutes its own class.

The original class is often referred to as the parent class or superclass of the newly created class. In addition, a subclass is sometimes referred to as a "specialization" of its superclass. Conversely, a superclass is a "generalization" of its subclasses.

Most importantly, inheritance promotes reuse. A developer can leverage existing software resources by reusing an existing group of classes which have similar behavior to that sought in a new program. This option assumes orderly, easily accessed class libraries which can be quickly perused by software developers.

When accessing a class named Dog, for example, a subclass called Hound might be built to define some hound-specific message such as RACE. Similarly, the class Dog could have a superclass constructed named Domestic Animal, of which Dog is only one instance. In both cases, most of the original class attributes are inherited by the new offspring.

Much of the craft of OOP lies in determining the most appropriate way to divide a program into an efficient aggregate of classes. This decision results in faster development time, proper class construction, and increased software reuse. Software reuse requires fewer lines of code, thus producing lower maintenance and fewer bugs in the software.

There are two basic inheritance vehicles in OOP – single inheritance and multiple inheritance. With single inheritance, a subclass may inherit methods and data from a single class while simultaneously adding or deleting behavior on its own. Multiple inheritance exists when a subclass can acquire methods and data from more than one class. These classes may be dispersed among different branches of a class hierarchy.

## Encapsulation and Polymorphism

Objects mask (or encapsulate) the internal structure of their data and the methods (or procedures) by which their functions work. Rather than baring these implementation details, objects present interfaces that represent their abstractions purely with no extraneous information. Thus, the principle of encapsulation frees the developer from knowing the inner workings of an object, as depicted in Figure 2.2.

## Figure 2.2 Object Encapsulation

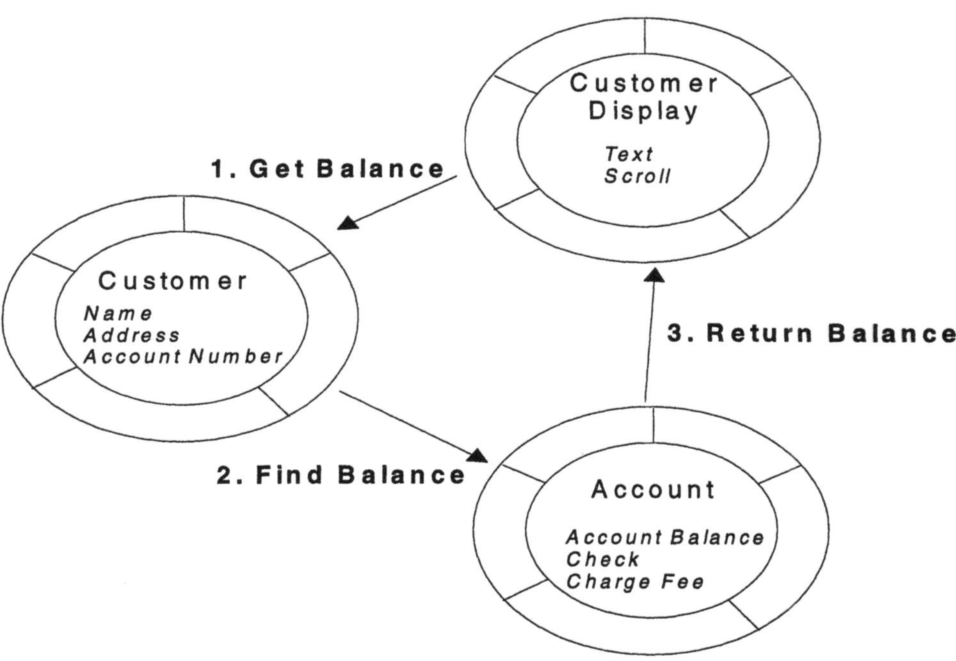


Because of encapsulation, for example, a programmer working with a bank account object need not comprehend the manner by which an object calculates its balance. The programmer is concerned solely with initiating the proper message, which elicits a balance from the appropriate object.

Should the organization modify the method for achieving balances, using applications will be unaffected because the specific methodology is encapsulated within an object or group of objects. Encapsulation thus creates intrinsic software modularity. Only the object's own methods can operate on the object's data. Messages from external objects invoke such internal operations.

Polymorphism takes encapsulation one step further. Its premise is "many shapes, one interface." A software component can make a request of another component without knowing precisely what that component is. The receiving component interprets the request, then determines how to execute the request according to its variables and data.

Polymorphism, therefore, provides a developer with the flexibility to create multiple definitions for functions. Creating multiple function definitions enables classes to be more generic and thus provide greater reusability. It also allows new components and functions to be added without disturbing the existing system.

Using a political analogy, polymorphism resembles "home rule." A central government, for example, may invoke a general mandate which says: "Maintain Order." This mandate is communicated to all the political subdivisions (states, provinces, and so forth) in the same manner, for one grand purpose: To Maintain Order. With home rule provisions in place, the actual implementation of this mandate is left to the devices and ingenuity of the individual political subdivisions.

Similarly, a generic command can be transmitted among several objects. The specific interpretation and implementation of such a command will depend on the properties of the object which receives the command. The generic Print command can result in one object producing text output while another displays graphic images. The result depends on the functionality resident within the object.

## Future Trends

In the long journey from machine languages to procedural programming, great strides were made in aiding the software development process. As time passed, however, application complexity increased in dramatic fashion. One of the more promising initiatives in object-oriented technology (OOT) has been the rise of frameworks to manage this complexity.

Frameworks represent one of the important trends for the future in object technology. However, they also represent an outgrowth of OO techniques which themselves evolved from earlier methodologies.

The idea is to design object classes that correspond to the essential features of a problem. Rather than fitting a problem to the procedural approach of a computer language, OOP allows the programmer to use the language to effectively model and solve real world problems. A drawing program, for example, might define classes that represent rectangles, polygons, and circles. The class definitions would include common functionality such as move and rotate which is the same for each class. A developer would then proceed, designing a program by deriving subclasses and overriding existing methods or implementing new methods within each class.

This approach allows developers to divide problems into small, manageable modules of code, where the principle of encapsulation insulates developers from the implementation details. Due to the principle of inheritance, developers can create a subclass to derive new classes from existing ones.

In addition, polymorphism provides the developer with the flexibility needed to create multiple definitions for functions. This flexibility allows classes to be more general and, as a result, more reusable. It also allows new components and functions to be added without disturbing the existing system. Implementing OOP makes it possible to design more extensible, reusable, and maintainable software.

By helping developers design and produce code more productively, the advantages of OOP have proven to outweigh those of traditional programming techniques. Even though the programming job is made easier because the developer works at a higher level of abstraction with objects and class libraries, the developer must still "put the pieces together." Simply changing from procedural techniques to OOP does not rectify the problem of providing infrastructure and extending functionality in a straightforward manner. Even with OOP, developers write extensive amounts of code because they continue to be responsible for providing the application's flow of control. Frameworks carry the OOP paradigm further by providing infrastructure and flexibility for deploying OOT.

Framework-oriented programming can be seen as the exploitation of OO frameworks to maximize the benefits of OOT. Although frameworks are not new to the software industry, they are creating quite a commotion in object technology circles. What exactly are frameworks? A widely accepted definition declares: "A framework is a set of classes that embodies an abstract design for solutions to a family of related problems."

Another way to define frameworks is: A prefabricated structure or template of a working program. For example, an application framework provides the support and "default" behavior for drawing windows, scroll bars, and menus, and controls the flow of events.

Frameworks are one of the more important advancements in OOT. Because frameworks provide infrastructure and flexible interfaces, they avoid the problems and overhead traditional programming imposes on developers. With well-designed frameworks, it is much easier to add extensions to factor out common functionality, enable interoperability, and improve software maintenance and reliability.

In general, the way frameworks achieve these benefits over other development approaches is based on two fundamental principles:

1. *Frameworks provide infrastructure and design* – Frameworks are not simply collections of classes. Rather, frameworks are adorned with rich functionality and strong "wired-in" interconnections between the object classes that provide an infrastructure for the developer. These interconnections provide the architectural model and design for developers and frees them to apply their expertise on the problem domain. By providing an infrastructure, the framework dramatically decreases the amount of standard code the developer must program, test, and debug. The developer writes only the code that extends or specifies the framework behavior to suit the program's requirements.

2. *Framework-oriented programming requires an organized thought process* – In procedural systems, the developer's own program provides all of the structure and flow of execution and makes calls to function libraries as necessary. The roles are reversed in framework-oriented programming, however. The role of the framework is to provide the flow of control, while

the developers need not be concerned with the details, and can focus their attention on their particular problem domain.

However, this change in control can carry significant ramifications for developers experienced only in procedural programming. The developer must learn to think in terms of the responsibilities of the object – what are the objects required to do – and let the framework determine when the objects should do what is required. Once the investment has been made to understand frameworks, developers will begin to realize the advantages framework-oriented programming can deliver over other development approaches.

# Business Benefits of Object-Oriented Technology

## Facilitating Software Development

There are two primary issues in software engineering that demand attention:

1.  Managing application complexity

2.  Improving programmer productivity

Object technology helps in both of these areas to a significant degree. There is no single cure-all solution available in the marketplace, however. Object techniques are but one, albeit important, part of the equation.

Software engineering has been accorded greater credibility because object technology has become prevalent. Objects provide an engineering-like discipline to the software development process. Prior to this, it was presumptuous to describe programming in engineering terms. It was more of a craft activity in its paltry reuse of previously created modules.

Object technology helps to manage complexity and increase productivity by encouraging development strategies, which include:

*   Write-reusable code

*   Sharing code with other routines

*   Writing easier-to-maintain code

---

- Improving legacy software modules

Object orientation represents a major shift in software development techniques and usage. Reusability, for example, implies that classes can be interchanged and modified to create new applications. The ability to encapsulate methods and data dramatically alters the programming process in terms of simplification, error prevention, and easier maintenance.

Simplification and the remainder of object technology's virtues only occur after the software practitioner undergoes an arduous learning experience. As has been affirmed many times, OO analysis, design, programming, and implementation are difficult for the novice. These procedures require adaptation to more abstract concepts than those encountered in the traditional programming world.

Once the principles and methods of object technology are absorbed, it becomes significantly easier to design and install OO applications because objects in the application domain map directly to objects in the software domain. This situation eliminates the need to convert a design to a conventional programming language which does not translate harmoniously in the same manner as objects.

The time and effort spent on programming will diminish once objects and class libraries are created and categorized, assuming a careful organization of these technical resources has been accomplished. Poorly defined and organized objects and class libraries will quickly erase the benefits of object technology.

The advantages of object techniques are particularly evident when assigning scarce technical personnel to new system developments. Large projects can be divided among members of a development team. Although this concept is certainly not new, object technology incorporates a difference.

In earlier pre-object years, the division of work among team members was a common occurrence. There was an important additional issue that warranted careful treatment: System integration. Numerous disparate software modules had to be carefully harmonized to produce an efficient, working system.

In the object world, independent developers build new classes from existing classes. All newly created subclasses are spawned by pre-existing classes through the property of inheritance. Consistency is provided because new objects and classes are generated from common parent classes. Finally, less coding is needed because existing modules are leveraged in the object creation task.

## Software Reuse

Successful implementation of a software reuse program in any organization is always dependent on the level of planning and support invoked in this process by technology management. If a reuse policy is allotted high priority such as by building a library of viable reuse components that are easy and safe to utilize, success may be achieved. Otherwise, developers will lack faith in the efficiency and reliability of stored software routines.

OOT particularly lends itself to reusability because of its inherent attributes of encapsulation, inheritance, and polymorphism. There is no guarantee, however, that software reuse will be achieved just because objects are part of the environment. Strong planning and support are essential to this process. There are several steps that will enhance reusability during the software development cycle:

- Strongly emphasize the importance of software reuse at the projects inception and continue to advocate its importance throughout. This step assumes the appropriate repository infrastructure has been implemented to support access to stored routines.

- Reuse planning must become a top priority of the software development process, similar in importance to selecting a database module, for example.

- As new software modules are created during the development process, evaluate their applicability to future reuse. Catalog and document their functionality for this future reuse.

- Create an integration plan that enables developers to easily synthesize reusable modules into a work-in-progress. Such a plan should create a seamless methodology for incorporating existing software modules.

- Insist that ongoing project review activities place strong emphasis on an analysis of the software reusability process. Consider to what degree it has been achieved and what changes, if any, are needed to strengthen reuse possibilities.

Final project documentation and deliverables must include detailed information on reuse policies employed in the project, in addition to guidelines and system documentation that supports future reuse of this software.

Not all software components are appropriate for a reuse policy, as their characteristics are not amenable to the process. Reusability must be invoked on a selective basis. It is too costly to simply catalog and save each new software module created during the development cycle. A careful implementation of a software reuse library insures its integrity and long term viability.

Successful reuse policies often proceed with no more than a few hundred modules stored. They all posses the essential attributes of universality that initially made them candidates for reuse. What is "universal" to one enterprise may not be so in another. Often, the measurement of a software module's appropriateness for reuse is based on the type of data with which it contends.

Some popular examples of reusable software components include audit routines, error handling, data access, GUI routines, security routines, utilities, help modules, and query routines. These examples represent only a small sample of reusability candidates. Each organization will develop its own criteria in this regard.

The numerous proponents of module reusability believe this process represents the next wave of software engineering. Object technology will play a featured role in this scenario because of its particularly appropriate characteristics for module reusability activities.

Reuse planning will inhabit every phase of the development cycle. It will play a role when incorporating existing components and will manage future reuse issues when new software modules are created.

While it is obvious reuse is a desirable goal, it is not always achieved in the day-to-day world of software development. There are various reasons for this:

- One reason is part of the human equation. Developers get paid to produce new code, not to tap into existing libraries. Should developers tap too frequently into existing libraries, management will begin to examine pay scales. Claude Monet was paid for painting new works, not for incorporating other people's art into a melange of artistic impressions.

- Another barrier to reuse is insufficient tools to augment the process. A few vendors are working in this area, but they are primarily small organizations still attempting to gain market recognition. One such vendor is ObjectSpace, Inc. of Houston. Another is Learmoth and Burchett Management Systems (LBMS), Inc. of Houston.

ObjectCatalog from ObjectSpace is a comparatively new product which provides developers with a capability to document, store, and locate an object. ObjectCatalog initiates a system for orderly reuse. The LBMS offering, entitled Project Engineer, presents a similar capability that focuses on storage methodologies.

Despite these early stirrings of tool availability, many implementation groups fail to emphasize reusability – particularly across project lines. These groups may feature object technology throughout the computing process, but expend minimal effort on reuse issues. They are far more interested in the adaptability of objects, the ability to change a system as the business model evolves.

It appears that object reuse needs another improvement, perhaps by development of a high-level language that supports the categorization, browsing, and testing of objects which have been stored in a repository. Some tool vendors are currently working on this capability.

Although the possibility of learning yet one more language is daunting, the payback of software reuse is considerable. Some of the large computer installations will introduce a new job specialty for the purpose of insuring efficient object reuse. These specialists will focus on software component management as opposed to the conventional software development function.

It is apparent, therefore, that creation of a well constructed object library – sometimes referred to as a repository – is critical to the success of object technology in general and software reusability in particular. There are several concerns that such a library should address. Among them:

- *Object Reuse* – An object's functionality and interface specifications must be easily determined when sought by project designers. Whatever the nature of the object, it must be located in a consistent fashion and there should be no ambiguity as to its purpose.

- *Open Design* – To the maximum extent possible, generic solutions should be applied to the process. Failure to utilize technologies such as CORBA, OLE, OpenDoc, SOM or DSOM will generate excessive amounts of work when the library must be rebuilt as a result of changing technology. Using standard methodologies – whether de facto or de jure in nature – can alleviate much of the problems associated with shifting industry trends.

- *Software Implementation* – When saving objects, it is important to record module interrelationships. Such information enhances software reuse by placing an object "in context" – few objects operate in a vacuum. There often are numerous interdependencies which, if known, can clarify the potential utility of any specific object for a particular application.

Object reusability does not come without a cost, however. It has been estimated that reusable objects are at least twice as expensive to build than those built for a specific purpose because of the need to plan for future contingencies when reusability is sought. In other words, it is faster and less expensive to create special purpose entities for the short-term and not worry about the future than it is to build a broad-based object.

Organizational structure relative to object creation and reuse often results in the creation of two distinct teams. There is an "object build" unit and another group that uses these objects to develop operational software modules. Initially, the object build team garners most of the attention because no software can be generated without an object inventory. Later, object users begin to develop software solutions. This delivery results in their ascendancy in the organizational hierarchy.

Reusability is the key element used to increase productivity. At the same time, reusability manages an escalating level of complexity. Classes encapsulate segments of code so complex tasks can be divided into manageable modules. The property of inheritance enables methods to be propagated from classes down to objects. All of these steps aid the search for reusable modules.

## Productivity Gains

One of the more challenging tasks for developers in this object-transition era is getting objects on the front-end to interact with relational databases on the back-end. This does not imply that OODBMS products will be unsuccessful. Rather, the problem lies in the many legacy relational packages already in use.

One approach, which it is representative of other approaches, is shown in Figure 3.1. Sybase's SQL Server database can be used with object technology because of middleware called Object Connect. Initially developed by Sybase to handle their own SQL Server database/object interaction, the tools also are being expanded to work with other databases.

### Figure 3.1 Sybase Middleware to Marry Objects to Databases

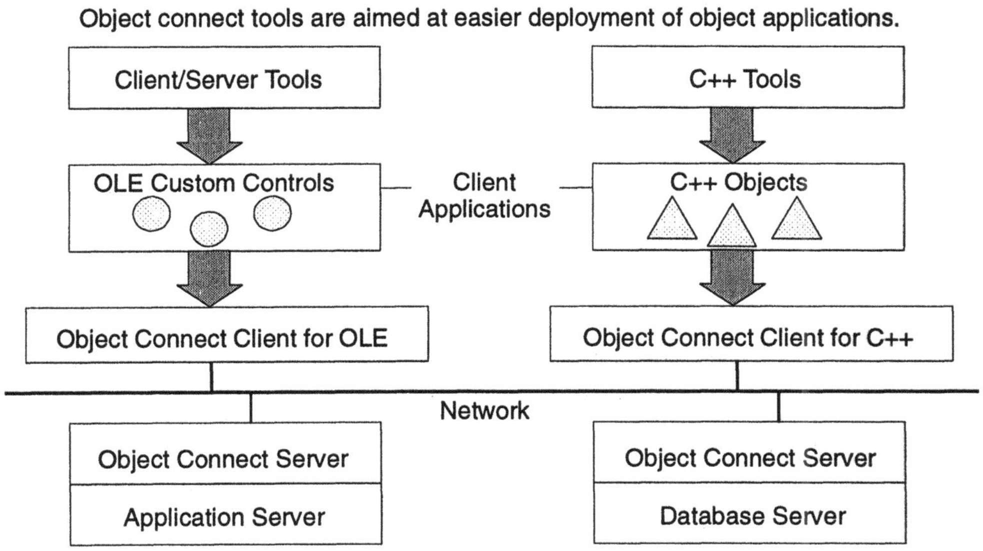

Object Connect for C++ enables programmers to build custom applications that utilize back-end databases. Object Connect for OLE performs the same function for Windows-based OLE applications. Prior to the arrival of tools such as Object Connect, developers often had to seek obscure third-party mechanisms to access relational databases from object-based applications.

Object Connect Server, also from Sybase, is a CORBA-compliant package that runs on application servers and allows objects to access other servers distributed throughout an organization. Oracle's Sedona offering presents a similar functionality. In their approach, objects within Oracle development tools can invoke functional mapping to databases and objects stored on distributed servers.

The middleware described is a helpful tool in the final analysis, but represents only an interim solution. The next advance will feature integrated support for objects within relational databases. At the same time, object databases will find their way into the enterprise, although at a more modest pace. Enterprises will directly support objects in all their manifestations.

Examples of other software enhancements that foster improved developer productivity are legion. Microsoft's ubiquitous development tool Visual Basic, for example, has added support for Network OLE. Figure 3.2 illustrates the omnipresent nature of Visual Basic in the marketplace.

## Figure 3.2 Visual Basic Marketplace Presence

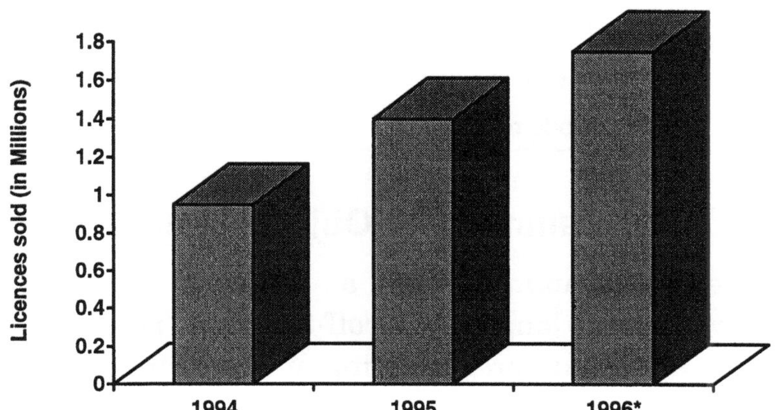


* Estimated

OLE Automation allows developers to physically segment an application into partitions and distribute them to other platforms. Developers need not be concerned about connection to different machines. The only OLE requirement: They know the name of the machine, what protocol is used, and what security levels are in place.

Network OLE offers compliance with OMG's CORBA and also allows developers to dynamically allocate and reallocate resources without networking existing applications. Other desired features for development tools are listed in table 3.1.

## Table 3.1 Tool List Attributes

- ◆ Cross-platform capabilities
- ◆ Collaboration tools
- ◆ Deployment control
- ◆ Configuration management
- ◆ Application partitioning
- ◆ Three-tier support
- ◆ Distributed-computing support

> ◆ Load and balance modeling
>
> ◆ Computer-aided software engineering
>
> ◆ Parallelism through threading
>
> ◆ Business process encapsulation
>
> ◆ Code reuse

## Programming by Object Masters

Today's advanced programmers use a startling array of tools, from sophisticated development languages to off-the-shelf "power packages." Some of these packages involve no programming at all; instead, they are intuitive in nature.

With OO programming, developers may not perceive their work as resembling conventional programming tasks because the techniques required to build OO applications will involve people who are not programmers in the traditional sense. There are sufficient operational procedures and knowledge built-in to models and class libraries so users will be able to design and implement many applications – particularly at the introductory level. Content-rich class libraries that represent real-world processes are the most valuable element of object technology.

Some of the commercial products now available are illustrative of development trends. One tool, for example, allows programmers to combine several object standards. Entitled Elements 2.x from Neuron Data, Inc. of Mountain View, California, it acts as a facilitator for CORBA, OLE, and OpenDoc components within the same application or applications. Elements 2.x also supports C++, the World Wide Web (the Web), and other objects by utilizing advanced object servers.

These servers resolve interactions among conflicting object standards. This open development environment enables Elements-based programs to possess all the virtues of objects and open systems themselves, namely portable, reusable, and interoperable. Only a cataclysmic change in object technology would change this.

  

Elements 2.x allows disparate objects to be incorporated within a single application. This degree of universality may not be necessary for every user, but can be useful in advanced application development. The product runs on Windows, OS/2, Solaris, and a growing range of platforms.

OO application packages, which require minimal fine-tuning, are assuming greater importance in enterprise environments. Each of these packages presents a specific functional focus. Vendors such as Marcam Corp., System Software Associates, Dun & Bradstreet Software, Inc., and Sherpa Corp. are early innovators in this area. IBM and Microsoft also are about to enter the arena.

Marcam's Protean, for example, is a production and inventory software package. PepsiCo, Inc. is an early implementor of Protean. Using several hundred Windows PCs, PepsiCo intends to link all of its North American bottling activities into a common system for controlling production and inventory of its commercial offerings. Object technology enables the company to enact system changes quickly without major upheavals.

# Chapter 4

# Object-Oriented Database Management Systems

## Background and Benefits

There have been three generations of data management models since the information age began in earnest. As shown in Figure 4.1, the Conference on Data System Languages (CODASYL) era prospered until the 1980s. CODASYL presented an orderly way of representing data in languages such as COBOL.

## Figure 4.1 Three Generations of Data Management

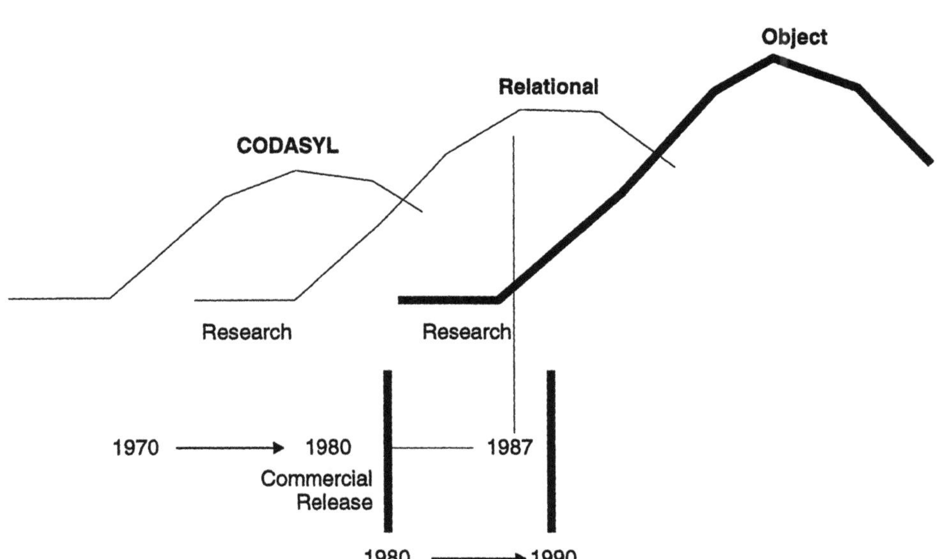

Beginning in the early 1980s and surging through the 1990s, RDBMS offerings emerged from obscurity. Object database products are continuing to rise on the growth curve and they will coexist with RDBMSs far into the future. Table 4.1 depicts some of the differentiations that exist between the relational and object models.

## Table 4.1 Database Technologies

| | Relational Data Model | Object Data Model |
|---|---|---|
| Definition | Data elements organized as relations and viewed as rows in a table | Data elements stored as objects that can contain complex data and procedures that can act on them |
| Basic Elements | Rows, columns, and tables | Objects, messages, and classes |
| Location of Procedures | In application | In objects |
| Typical Data Types | Text, numbers, and binary large objects (BLOBs) | Text, numbers, images, voice, and video |
| Typical Programming Languages | 4GLs, C, SQL | C++, Smalltalk |
| Typical Applications | Commercial, including OLTP, accounting, human resources, and sales tracking | Mostly technical, including CAD/CAM, MCAD, ECAD, GIS, CIM, CAP, and imaging |
| Anticipated Applications | Any commercial application, but especially OLTP | Office automation, financial modeling, and multimedia |
| Advantage | • Predominant data model in commercial applications today<br>• Mature, yet continuing to evolve | • Objects reusable and have inheritance<br>• Has ability to model real world |

The transition to OODBMS products parallels the overall changes in technology itself. As shown in Table 4.2, development tools such as programming languages have transitioned from raw assembler languages to more utilitarian high-level languages to current object languages such as C++ and Smalltalk. Object databases are also part of this migration and will continue to maintain their importance in the next century.

## Table 4.2 Object Transition

| | 1970s | 1980s | 1990s |
|---|---|---|---|
| User Interface | Punch cards, Teletype (TTY) | Character CRT | Object GUIs |
| Programming Language | ASM (assembler) | High-level languages (HLL), Fortran, C | Object Procedural Languages (PLs) – C++, Smalltalk |
| Storage Interface | Device Input/Output | Record Input/Output | Object DBMS |

Object databases were introduced in the late 1980s to provide database management for applications built using object technology. Object technology enhances traditional application development by introducing new data modeling and programming techniques. To achieve better code reuse and maintainability, object technology organizes code into objects, which combine data and procedures. This step introduces significant database issues because the object model is different from traditional data models in many respects.

The first set of capabilities that differentiate object databases from other databases is full OOP support. For developers using C++ or Smalltalk, the ability of an object database to support OOP using inheritance, polymorphism, and encapsulation simplifies application development because they must only work with one set of programming rules.

Object databases are designed to support the object models generated with these languages. The developer can directly store and retrieve objects and invoke methods. The object database does not restrict the developer's use of an object model or require the developer to translate the object model to another data model. The object database provides traditional database capabilities for the object model such as data independence and integrity.

When a developer uses an object model to encapsulate a set of data and associated methods, the specifics of the data structures are hidden. Published methods are used to access the information so applications are insulated from the particulars of the object's internal data structure. This insulation simplifies access and provides independence for the object because the internals can be modified without affecting external code.

An object database provides the same simplicity for storing and managing objects because the data and methods associated with the object are encapsulated and available in accordance with OOP rules. Applications access and operate with persistent objects stored in the object database using standard OO language semantics and operations. In contrast, relational database technology requires the developer to translate the object model to the supported data model and include routines to provide this mapping at runtime, involving additional development effort and reducing runtime performance.

Object databases also are designed to extend traditional database capabilities. They support nontraditional data types, direct navigational links between objects, flexible versioning, and transaction mechanisms. Object databases support these additional capabilities both because they are generally required by the object models because many new applications involve nontraditional data.

Multimedia is often used as an example of a nontraditional data type supported by object databases because it is of current interest. However, many traditional kinds of data such as graphics, geometry, and text have very similar characteristics. The object database storage model can store these directly in the database. Many applications edit and modify objects as dynamically varying objects. The ability for an object database to work with an object having a complex internal structure with changing storage requirements fits these applications much better than the normalized tabular data models provided by relational databases.

Direct navigational links between objects also are available for high performance access to individual objects. An application can traverse such a linkage directly from one object to any other object without requiring traditionally expensive operations such as relational table "joins," for example, links from one table entry to another. This provides access paths that are substantially faster than other database technologies.

Object databases also can store multiple versions of objects, with change histories that track modifications. An application can work with a specific version or even multiple versions of any object. This ability provides flexibility for applications in which a user may experiment with a variety of changes. This is a very different requirement than traditional databases address.

According to market researchers, the market for object database systems is the fastest growing segment of the software industry worldwide. Growing at a compound annual rate of more than 100% each year, the market will exceed $950 million by 1998. In fact, in its brief history, the market has at least doubled every year – a growth rate significantly faster than the early years of the relational database market.

There are a number of market dynamics propelling this growth:

- Rapid growth of OOP environments

- Rapid emergence of OO operating systems

- Demand for storage, distribution, and management of complex information

- Growth of the C/S market

- Emergence of new standards

The first of these market dynamics is the rapidly growing installed base of OOP languages such as C++ and Smalltalk. In most market areas, C++ has become the industry standard for OO development. The installed base of C++ compilers on PCs and workstations alone already totals well over one million. Microsoft's Visual C++ product is currently the fastest selling development environment in the industry, and every major computer vendor offers a robust OOP environment. The enormous installed base of programming environments is creating significant market pull for object database systems. In fact, there is a close correlation between sales of programming languages and object database systems. A typical scenario: An object database system is purchased as a repository for application objects after investing in an OOP language.

The rapid emergence of operating systems that use OO features is another major market force leading to the growth of object database systems. Whether it is the Mac, Microsoft's OLE and Cairo, Project DOE from Sun Microsystems, DOMF from HP or OS/2, System Object Model (SOM), and DSOM from IBM – all major operating systems are being redesigned to permit OO application development. In fact, objects are rapidly replacing computer files as the basic element of information in the 1990s.

Traditional CODASYL or relational databases have been optimized for simple, record-oriented data such as text and numerical information. Today, however, new applications have more demanding data models that require the managing of graphics, text, audio, video, and a wide variety of other digital information. These applications demand the richer and more flexible storage format than object database systems can provide. Companies are moving to object database systems to store, distribute, and manage the more complex information their new applications demand.

Perhaps the industry's strongest trend is the growth of the C/S application market. Referred to as downsizing, rightsizing or smartsizing, developers are off-loading applications from their central systems and distributing them in networks of PCs and workstations. With their history firmly rooted in the centralized computing domain, CODASYL and relational databases have only partially moved to the world of C/S computing, despite the marketing attention. Conversely, because most object database system architectures were developed only recently, nearly 90% of all object database system applications execute in a C/S environment.

Many of these C/S applications require groupware support. Once again, while traditional databases support very fast access to simple record-oriented information, their transaction model limits the effectiveness of sharing data in a group. Object database systems offer product features which allow users to collaborate effectively in groups and increase productivity.

The final trend propelling the market for object databases is the widely available set of industry standards for object software. The CORBA from the

OMG, the COM standard from Microsoft, the SOM standard from IBM, and ODMG's database standard are all in place and provide a road map for software developers. Object database applications can now be developed in compliance with a standard set of interfaces.

Object database systems have become successful in markets where traditional databases cannot provide a satisfactory solution. For example, object databases provide the necessary features that applications such as ECAD mechanical computer-aided design (MCAD), computer-aided software engineering (CASE), and geographic information systems (IS) have not found elsewhere. Many of these applications must migrate data from a proprietary data management system or file system. Because object database systems provide interactive access to information in a C/S environment, they are a natural partner for these graphically oriented applications. Figure 4.2 outlines the growth of object databases across the C/S management information systems (MIS), business reengineering, telecommunications, and engineering design segments.

## Figure 4.2 Object Database Growth

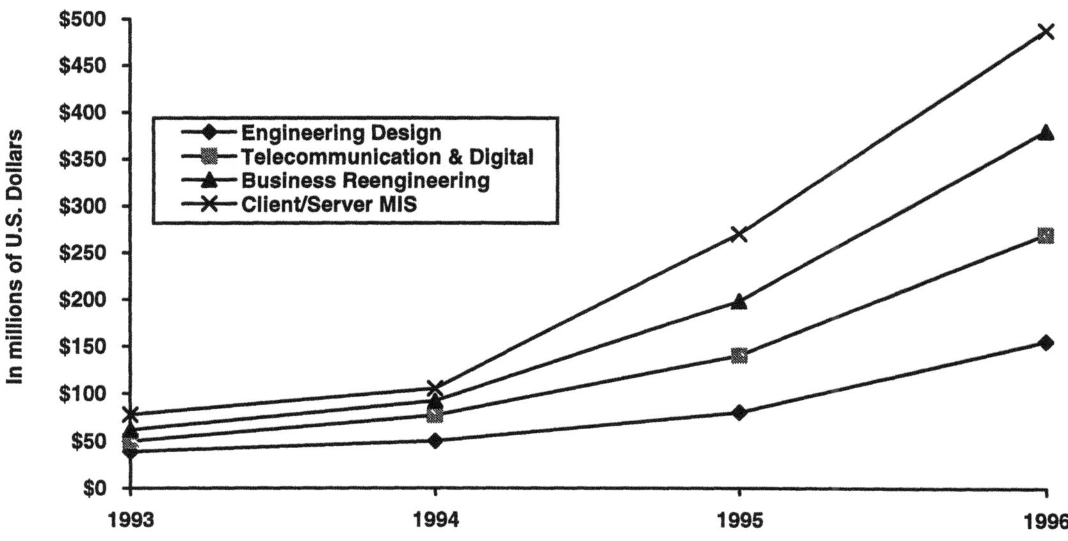


As the engineering design market continues to grow steadily in the years ahead, new market segments emerge and grow rapidly. As Figure 4.2 illustrates, engineering design was initially the largest segment of the market, but other segments are showing signs of meeting and exceeding the engineering design segment.

The second major market for object databases has been in telecommunications. Relational database applications already exist in applications including customer service, billing, and financial services, but the requirements of audio and visual information has exceeded the capacities of conventional databases. As this trend continues worldwide, the telecommunications, broadcasting, and cable industries are creating a digital pathway for access to information required for interactive television (TV), personal phone services, and online database access services. Managing this information will require new applications with rich data types that demand the performance of an OO database.

As corporations reinvent themselves to compete more effectively in the global economy, they are reengineering many of their applications around process flow rather than functional organization. A typical example of a business reengineering application is the effective management of a customer order from sales to manufacturing, shipping, customer support, and marketing. Reorganizing processes such as these typically mean managing compound documents or other digital images across multiple computer architectures, financial systems, and locations. Object database systems provide the storage and distribution mechanism to manage this new kind of information flow.

The final major market for object databases is in commercial C/S systems. Even traditional financial analysis, decision support, taxation, insurance, and billing applications are being upgraded to handle more detailed and query-based information. Financial applications have an increasing need to handle time-sensitive information that is best presented in a graphical format. Customer service applications are being redesigned to include access to online catalogs or routing systems for service personnel. Many of these applications are graphical, geographic or voice annotated as a way of improving information access.

## Object-Oriented Database Functions

On the road to full object-orientation, there are some caveats that should be noted. Some OODBMS offerings, particularly in the early years, attempted to present themselves as OO products, while only adding minor improvements to older modules. For example, one approach featured an OO user interface, but retained the old data storage technique of tabular data formats underneath. This approach has a debilitating effect on system performance.

When modeling a prospective OO system, there are several areas that must be examined carefully. These are inheritance, object embedding, object grouping, and object relationships.

- *Inheritance* – A type of relationship between different kinds of objects. It allows one kind of object to share the structure or behavior defined in one (single inheritance) or more (multiple inheritance) other kinds of objects. Inheritance is one of the most important concepts in object-orientation because it provides a means to reuse and extend previously defined objects.

- *Object embedding* – The ability to have one object contained within another object. This is a common technique used in modeling objects. Some object database systems may not provide this essential feature.

- *Object grouping* – This relates to an object that groups together other objects. Object-orientated applications require the capability to group objects into a single logical container without actually copying or modifying the objects. These collections are abstract structures that resemble arrays in programming languages or tables in a relational database.

- *Relationships* – They are the key to modeling complex objects such as designs, hierarchies, documents, and multimedia information. Each relationship is composed of two or more relationship pointers that are constrained to be consistent with one another in a particular fashion. Users determine the constraints on the data members composing the relationship.

Most organizations planning the move from procedural to OO technology have a large investment in legacy code. They cannot afford to simply ignore this valuable resource. There are several criteria that must be considered. These issues are important markers for determining the scope of the task involved with code conversion:

- What percentage of existing code must be modified? (This figure should be in the low single digits.)

- Are the objects in the OODBMS compatible with libraries in other languages being used?

- What level of difficulty is involved with converting existing data?

- Is the object system flexible and transparent enough to permit using another package if conditions warrant?

The object database systems market is experiencing its next generation of products. Some first-generation object database systems were based on proprietary languages which have already become obsolete. Other products were based on special-purpose application languages such as LISP. Perhaps the most important trend in software development is the emergence of C++ as one of the industry standard OO languages. When evaluating products, note these attributes: Support for virtual functions, parameterized types, all C and C++ data types, and persistence independent of type.

In addition, note the degree of support for virtual functions that can be inherited and overridden to offer different behavior to ensure the complete benefits of encapsulation and inheritance in C++ are supported. Some object database system products cannot support basic OO concepts such as virtual base classes and multiple inheritance.

Parameterized types help users build libraries of reusable software. Support for all C++ data types, not just a few of the common types such as character and integer, should be provided. Some OO databases cannot store classes which contain pointers, unions, and other important C++ types and type constructors. In such a case, existing class libraries must be rewritten to allow persistence for objects.

Most advanced object database systems use a method for storing objects in which persistence is not part of the type of an object; this is known as persistence independent of type. Persistence for data structures should be independent of its type so the same data descriptions can work unmodified with both transient and persistent data. The key to ease-of-use – particularly when using OOP techniques – is in the integration between the database system and the host programming language.

In the final analysis, the criteria for OO languages must offer a minimum level of attributes. Among those attributes are support for:

- Virtual functions

- Virtual base classes

- Single and multiple inheritance

- All major C++ data types

- Persistence independent of type

Any worthwhile database must provide a robust query capability. The synergy between SQL and relational databases is well established. A similar, if not identical, union must be available when utilizing OODBMS packages. Some of the features needed in this environment are distributed query capability and an optimization mechanism.

To allow programmers to provide query expressions that select the objects of interest based on the values contained in the object, object database systems must support associative retrieval or queries across sets of objects. In a distributed C/S environment, it is common to have a database distributed across multiple servers. A query should be able to span multiple databases and multiple servers.

Some object database systems have query languages based on the syntax of SQL, but provide different semantics. Thus, these query languages create the illusion of SQL capability, but bear little resemblance to real SQL. Furthermore, most of these implementations are limited in basic functions. For example, multi-attribute, multiple condition queries are missing from many of these products. Others are limited to performing all queries only for class extents. Others do not support queries nested in other queries.

Because object database system queries can be arbitrarily complex, the query language should be functionally complete, including the ability to declare variables, make use of pointers or addresses of any kind and call functions or member functions in the query. The ideal query languages for querying object database systems are based on the full capability of the host object language.

An object query facility should provide an optimizer that examines a variety of strategies and chooses the most efficient method to execute a query. The approach used by the optimizer should allow for flexibility at run-time, yet carry out analysis of the query at compile-time. To minimize network traffic, indexes should be used to reduce the number of objects moved to the client. Indexes in an object query system should be more functional than indexes in a relational database because they may need to index paths through objects and collections, not just fields directly contained in objects.

## Products

There are nearly 25 OODBMS products in the commercial arena and the numbers continues to grow. Some are "pure" object systems, while others are hybrid object/relational offerings. Two representatives in the "pure" category are ObjectStore from Object Design, Inc. of Burlington, Massachusetts and Objectivity/DB from Objectivity, Inc. of Mountain View, California.

ObjectStore is an OODBMS which implements a full OO data model and offers tightly-integrated language interfaces to a set of traditional DBMS features including persistence, transaction management (concurrency control and recovery), distributed access, associative queries over large amounts of data, and database administration utilities. The system supports programming language interfaces for C, C++, and Smalltalk, and comes with a graphical, interactive schema designer; incremental compilation and linking facilities; source-level debugging; and a graphical, interactive database browser. ObjectStore supports C++ extensions providing data manipulation (query support). ObjectStore is supported on Sun, HP, IBM, Digital Equipment Corp., Silicon Graphics, Inc. (SGI) UNIX platforms, Windows, OS/2, and Novell NetWare PC platforms.

ObjectStore uses a C/S architecture that allows one server to support many client workstations, each workstation to simultaneously access multiple databases on many servers, and a server to be resident on the same machine as a client. This architecture is shown in Figure 4.3.

## Figure 4.3 ObjectStore Architecture

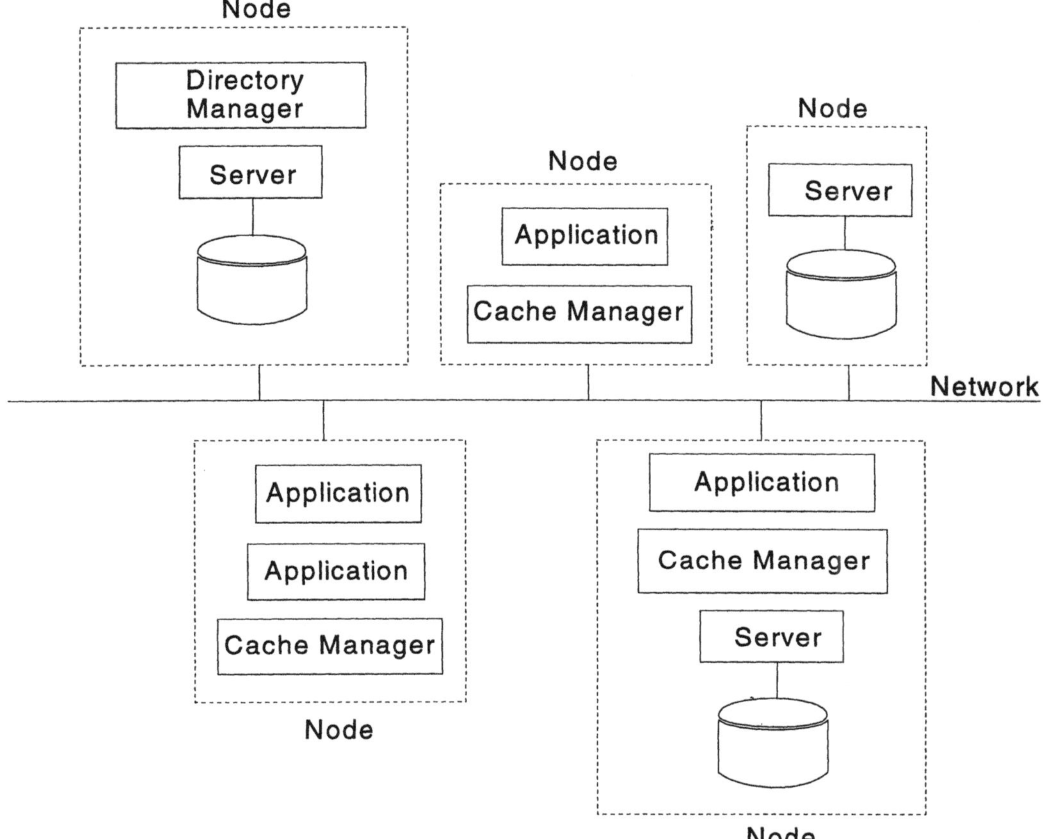


The product executes an ObjectStore server process on every machine which acts as a database server. The ObjectStore server provides a long-term repository for persistent data. Objects are stored on the server in the same format in which they are seen by the application in virtual memory, which avoids overhead in moving between different persistent and transient forms of the object. Objects can cross page boundaries and can be much larger than a page, and the server stores and retrieves pages of data in response to requests from clients. The server knows nothing about page contents; it simply passes pages to and from the client and stores them on disk. The server also is responsible for concurrency control and recovery, using techniques similar to those used in conventional DBMS. The server provides two-phase locking with a read-write lock for each page in addition to back-up to long-term storage media such as tapes. While recovery is based on a logging protocol, transactions involving more than one server are coordinated using a two-phase commit protocol. With two-phase commit, a coordinating database ensures every database involved in a transaction update makes necessary updates or none of them do. The database servers advise the coordinating database of their ability to update. If all respond affirmatively, the updates occur. Otherwise, the entire transaction is cancelled.

ObjectStore executes a cache manager process on each client machine. The cache manager participates in the management of an application's client cache, a local holding area for data mapped or waiting to be mapped into the application's virtual memory. Only one cache manager is executed on a client machine, even if multiple clients are executed. The server and client communicate via LANs when they are running on different hosts and by faster facilities such as shared memory and local sockets when they are running on the same host. ObjectStore's distributed architecture supports several network environments for interoperability among popular workstations and PCs, and includes support for transmission control protocol/Internet protocol (TCP/IP), Novell internetwork packet exchange/sequenced packet exchange (IPX/SPX), and other popular network protocols.

Rather than storing databases as regular files managed by the OS, databases may also be stored in special ObjectStore file systems managed by an ObjectStore Directory Manager. These file systems have a logical organization which is independent of that of any OS file system.

ObjectStore attempts to present the application programmer with the appearance of a single object space consisting of both transient and persistent objects, rather than forcing the programmer to manage separate application and database memory spaces and explicit movement of data between them, as in relational database application programs. Thus, deferencing pointers to persistent objects and cache coherency is entirely managed by the system, transparently to the programmer. Moreover, ObjectStore's architecture adheres to a primary goal to make the speed of deferencing pointers to persistent objects be the same as that of deferencing pointers to transient objects based on the requirements of CAD and similar applications. This function is completed once the persistent object has been retrieved from the database.

ObjectStore's goal: There should be no additional overhead required to determine whether the object pointed to by a pointer being deferenced has already been retrieved from the database. To accomplish this goal, ObjectStore takes advantage of OS interfaces that allow virtual memory access violations to be handled by ordinary software. These interfaces are available in most standard versions of UNIX and other kernel-based operating systems such as OS/2.

These virtual memory interfaces allow ObjectStore to set protection for any page of virtual memory to no access, read-only or read-write. When an ObjectStore application dereferences a pointer whose target object has not been retrieved into the client (for example, a page set to no access), the hardware detects an access violation and the OS passes this to ObjectStore as a memory fault. As noted, ObjectStore maintains a client cache consisting of a pool of database pages that have recently been used in the virtual memory of the client host. When the application signals a memory fault, ObjectStore determines whether the page being accessed is in the client cache. If not, it asks the ObjectStore server to transmit the page to the client and puts the page into the client cache. Once the page is in the client cache, ObjectStore calls the OS to set the protection of the page to read-only to permit access. ObjectStore then returns from the memory fault, causing the dereference to restart and succeed.

Subsequent reads to the same target object – or to other addresses on the same page – will run in a single instruction without causing a fault. Writes to the target page will result in faults that cause the page access mode and lock in order to be upgraded to read-write. Because a page can reside in the client cache without being locked, some other client might modify the page in the database, invalidating the cached copy. A cache coherency mechanism involving the use of callback messages between clients is used to ensure transactions always view valid copies of pages. All virtual memory mapping and address space manipulation in the application is handled by the OS under the direction of ObjectStore, using normal system calls.

Additionally, ObjectStore databases can exceed the size of the virtual address space; two independent databases might each use the same addresses for their own objects. ObjectStore contains mechanisms for managing these problems. Specifically, ObjectStore dynamically assigns portions of address space to correspond to portions of the databases used by the application, and also maintains a virtual address map that shows which database and which object within the database is represented by an address. As the application references more databases and more objects, additional address space is assigned and the new objects are mapped into these new addresses. At the end of each transaction, the virtual address map is reset. When the next transaction starts, new assignments are made. Each transaction is limited to accessing no more data than can fit into the virtual address space.

Although ObjectStore attempts to maintain a single object space abstraction for the application programmer, there are a number of aspects of the mapping that the programmer must be aware of. Specifically, the inter-object pointers that can appear in an ObjectStore program fall into different categories, and different validity considerations apply to pointers from these categories:

- Transient memory to transient memory

- Persistent memory in one database to persistent memory in the same database

- Persistent memory in one database to persistent memory in another database

- Transient memory to persistent memory

- Persistent memory to transient memory

Pointers in the first two categories are always valid. Pointers in the last three categories are valid only until the end of the current transaction. The validity restriction on the last two categories are inherent in any mapping from a shared persistent object space (the database) to a private transient object space (the application program). The validity restriction for the last category has to do with the way ObjectStore handles multiple databases.

Generally speaking, an OODBMS's concurrency control mechanism guarantees copies of database objects mapped into the application's object space, and the corresponding objects in the persistent database are synchronized within a transaction. When the transaction ends, changes made to persistent objects by the application are written back into the database, and those objects are made available to other concurrently-executing applications.

Pointers from persistent memory to transient memory become invalid outside a transaction because they are not usable by other applications accessing the shared database (they are local to the application), and the DBMS cannot guarantee the object pointed to by the reference has not been moved by the client, deleted by the application or exists (the application may no longer be running). Pointers from transient memory to persistent memory become invalid outside a transaction because the persistent objects may move or be deleted by a concurrent application.

ObjectStore's clustering facility allows objects to be explicitly clustered to raise the probability that objects likely to be accessed from a given object are moved to application memory together, and thus already are in memory when referenced. For example, if all components of a parts assembly are clustered together, the first reference to one of the components causes the entire assembly to be cached in the client memory; subsequent references to components are processed at memory speed. The programmer can specify objects are to be allocated to a given database, to a specified segment of a database or to a specific cluster with a segment. ObjectStore provides a specific access policy with a given segment. This provision controls how much of the segment will be moved from the server to the client if an object in the segment is referenced, and the object is not already located at the client.

The product supports traditional database transactions employing two-phase locking, additional forms of transactions required in complex applications such as "long" and "nested" transactions, and notification between users and other forms of cooperation among applications. Two-phase locking resembles two-phase commit. It is a two-step process to lock data while updates occur. ObjectStore also provides support for object versioning and configurations, and supports full online back-up for continuous processing environments.

ObjectStore/DBConnect is designed to provide interfaces between ObjectStore and other database systems. Interfaces provided include:

- Disk management

- Performance monitoring

- Back-up and recovery

- Security and access control

ObjectStore also supports query access to collections of objects in addition to access using direct object references typically required by design applications. Queries treat persistent and non-persistent data in a uniform manner.

Indexes can be defined over collections of objects and are used by ObjectStore's query optimizer to improve the efficiency of queries, as in a RDBMS. However, in ObjectStore, indexes are not restricted to data members (attributes) of the members of a collection. Indexes may also be defined on paths (series of data members that span multiple objects) that may be frequently searched.

The query facilities are based on the idea that database searching will be done primarily by navigation (following object references) from other persistent objects using object-valued properties or by queries performed over explicitly-defined collection objects that play the role of type or class extensions. The system supports persistent variables (called roots) that can name either individual or collection objects and can thus act as named entry points into databases.

Objectivity/DB is a C/S DBMS from Objectivity, Inc. Its placement within the overall database marketplace is reflected in Table 4.3. The table illustrates Objectivity/DB (ODB) is particularly appropriate for applications that require a flexible information model, involve complex relationships, and generally demand high performance.

## Table 4.3 Relational and Object Database Markets

| DBMS Segments | Engineering and Technical | Technical and Advanced Information Systems | Mainstream Information Systems |
|---|---|---|---|
| Applications | Engineering, scientific, design automation, simulation | Groupware, multimedia, logistics, operations, network management, manufacturing, process control, document imaging | Financial, OLTP, order entry, financial accounting |
| Characteristics | ♦ Tactical, language-oriented, OO languages, UNIX<br><br>♦ Complex information model, simple interaction model, single-user to small workgroups (limited concurrency) | ♦ Mission critical, database-oriented, OO languages, UNIX, and PCs<br><br>♦ Complex information model, complex integration model, small workgroups through enterprisewide systems | ♦ Mission critical, database-oriented, traditional languages<br><br>♦ Mainframes, UNIX, and PCs<br><br>♦ Simple information models, small interaction model, small workgroups through enterprisewide |
| Development Tools | Language compiler tools | Language compiler tools | 4GLs, etc. |
| Solutions | Persistent languages, OODBMS | Objectivity/DB | RDBMSs |

ODB offers a distributed C/S architecture that provides scalability while maintaining performance to the highest levels possible. It also supports the direct storage and management of objects through standard language interfaces. These languages include C++, Smalltalk, C, and SQL.

Interoperability across all major hardware platforms and operating systems is provided. An American National Standards Institute (ANSI)-standard SQL interface is included which permits users to utilize various C/S tools based on Microsoft's open database connectivity (ODBC) interface. Table 4.4 lists additional features.

## Table 4.4 Objectivity/Database Features and Benefits

| Objectivity/DB Feature | Benefits |
|---|---|
| Distributed C/S architecture | Scalable to gigabytes of objects |
| ANSI-standard SQL interface | Accessible by SQL |
| ODBC support | Accessible by popular C/S tools |
| Replicated objectbase services | Fault tolerance, support for WANs, object database partitioning |
| Complete interoperability across UNIX, Windows, Windows NT, OpenVMS, OSF/1 | Leverage of existing hardware investment, flexibility in future choices |
| Transparent C++ and Smalltalk bindings | Simple to add objectbase support to applications |
| Object cluster caching on client | High performance for object traversals |
| Location independence of objects | No application changes required as objects move across servers |
| Transparent to native file systems | Support for fault tolerant servers with mirrored disks |
| Object-level versioning | Support for collaborative computing applications |
| Locking options – read, write, multiple readers one write (MROW) | Flexible locking architecture for high performance |
| Object reference architecture | Guaranteed integrity for all ODB objects per the ODMG-93 specification |
| Long and short transactions | Choice for appropriate transaction type for all types of applications |
| Extensive administrative tools and API such as online back-up/restore, object relocation | Administrative capabilities for deployment of mission-critical applications |

As depicted in Figure 4.4, ODB is one of the more advanced OODBMS products serving the distributed C/S market. Its architectural approach solves many of the performance impediments seen in other offerings by moving database system services to the client process. This approach includes object caching, updates, traversals, and conversion operations for interoperability. The I/O services are moved to separate server processes on the machines where the data resides and a separate server process handles concurrency control.

## Figure 4.4 Comparison of Client/Server Architectures

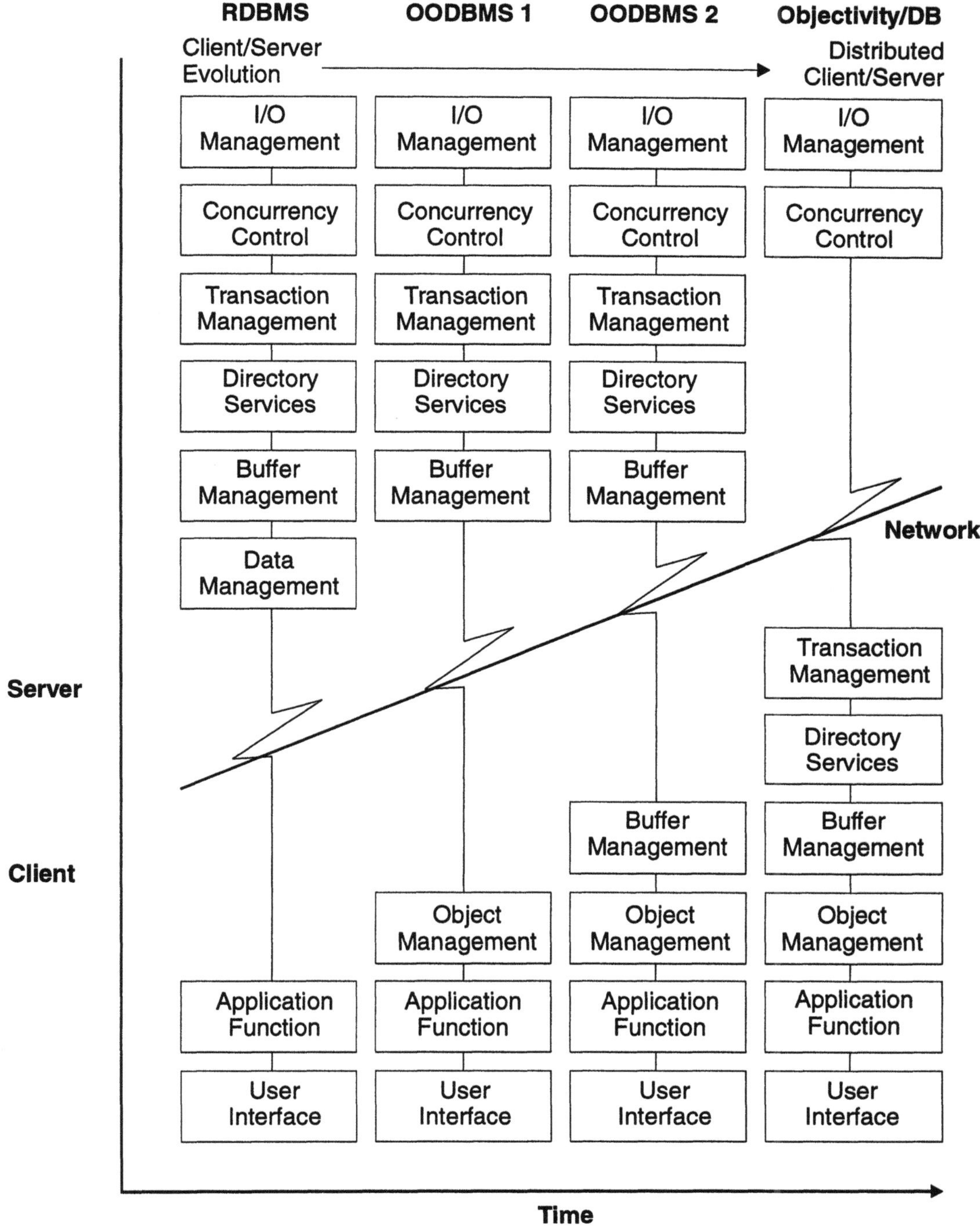

The balanced nature of this architecture enhances ODB scalability. Much of the computation is performed on the client, making efficient use of client CPU resources that server-dominant implementations fail to exploit. As a result, the ODB handles more client processes than achieved with server-dominant systems. The processing power and performance of the database increases as each new client platform is added to the system.

Scalability is the bane of object database products. Similar to early C/S systems themselves, object databases have gained notoriety for their lack of scalability. ODB's marriage with a newer, more scalable C/S architecture has transferred some of the positive attributes of this scalability to ODB itself.

Figure 4.5 shows an example of databases distributed across multiple servers and across multiple disks on a single server. These multiple servers share the processing load for server I/O operations, which eliminates the I/O processing slowdown that can occur when information is stored on a single disk server.

# Figure 4.5 Distributed Client/Server Architecture

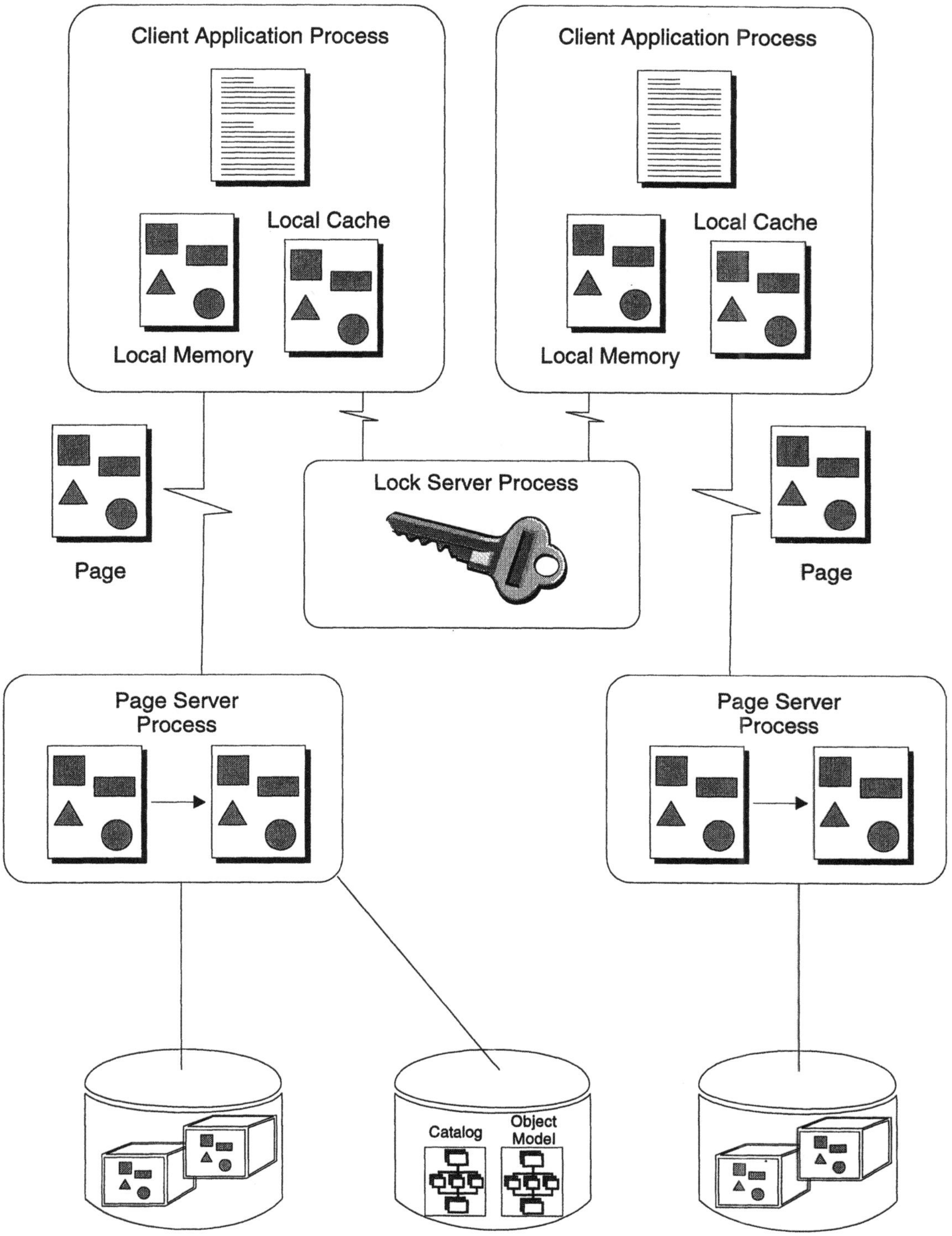

By using distributed servers, ODB can grow significantly in size and complexity while maintaining a linear performance profile. As a result, the product can support hundreds of thousands of objects spread physically across the enterprise. Applications can transparently access these enterprisewide objects without knowing where the objects actually reside.

ODB server processes perform page read and write operations, with one or more pages containing a cluster of objects. This approach is different from some other OODBMS, which read and write objects individually. These OODBMS access the server for every single object. But because network access can be many times slower than local access, the performance penalty for this OODBMS access is large. For applications where performance is important, users of such OODBMS are forced to explicitly read objects in groups to amortize this cost and simulate the clustered access the OODBMS could have performed transparently.

The ODB approach of reading objects as clusters and caching them on the client can improve performance because it reduces the number of times objects must be read from disk. In many cases, objects needed by an application will already reside in the client's cache.

ODB servers execute multiple I/O requests in parallel, even if the requested objects reside on the same machine. ODB uses a separate server to manage lock requests. This design allows I/O requests to be processed independently of lock requests. Even in single server environments where the server manages both locking and client I/O requests, the server can process lock requests concurrently with I/O operations. This ability eliminates performance bottlenecks caused when lock requests and I/O requests of a client process are forced to wait each time a server processes an I/O or lock request of another client process.

There are server machines specialized for I/O operations currently offered. They are not designed for CPU-intensive applications, and often do not allow user applications to run on them. Because ODB separates I/O services from the CPU-intensive system services, it can take advantage of these servers. ODB clients directly access high-speed I/O servers for their objects. Server-dominant systems must place their server on a different machine, and their clients are forced to access data indirectly through that third machine, losing some of the advantage of the I/O server.

ODB insures integrity of objects by using object references rather than direct pointers to access objects. This architectural difference, which follows the ODMG-93 guidelines, separates ODB from virtual memory-based ODBMS. For example, in virtual memory systems (VMS), direct pointers to objects become invalid after a transaction is committed. Pointers also are invalidated when an object is moved to another location in the address space. When another transaction dereferences one of these pointers, it will either cause the application to crash or possibly dereference the pointer into the middle of some other object at that physical pointer location. This scenario can cause object database corruption, which may go undetected for weeks or months. Recovery from this kind of corruption is difficult because countless database changes are lost in the time lag.

The amount of data a virtual memory-based OODBMS application can access in one transaction is limited by the pointer size of the host machine where the application is running. Typically, this size is 32-bits, which imposes a limit on accessible data. ODB has no limit. Any transaction can transparently and simultaneously access all data in an object database through 64-bit object references, which allows users to access up to virtually unlimited objects.

ODB provides interoperability among different architectures and operating systems, including Windows NT, Windows 3.1, Windows for Workgroups 3.11, UNIX, and OpenVMS. These architectures can be used as clients, servers or both. Objects can be distributed and freely moved across different server architectures and shared among different kinds of clients. The product transparently handles inherent differences between these architectures such as byte order, floating point format, and packing and padding alignment. ODB translates on the object level only when necessary.

As shown in Figure 4.6, the physical locations of objects are transparent to ODB applications, allowing users to locate and relocate objects on any machine without changing applications that access them. For example, for performance reasons users may want to move certain objects to a client machine that accesses them most often. If access patterns to these objects change, the objects can be moved again.

## Figure 4.6 Location Independence

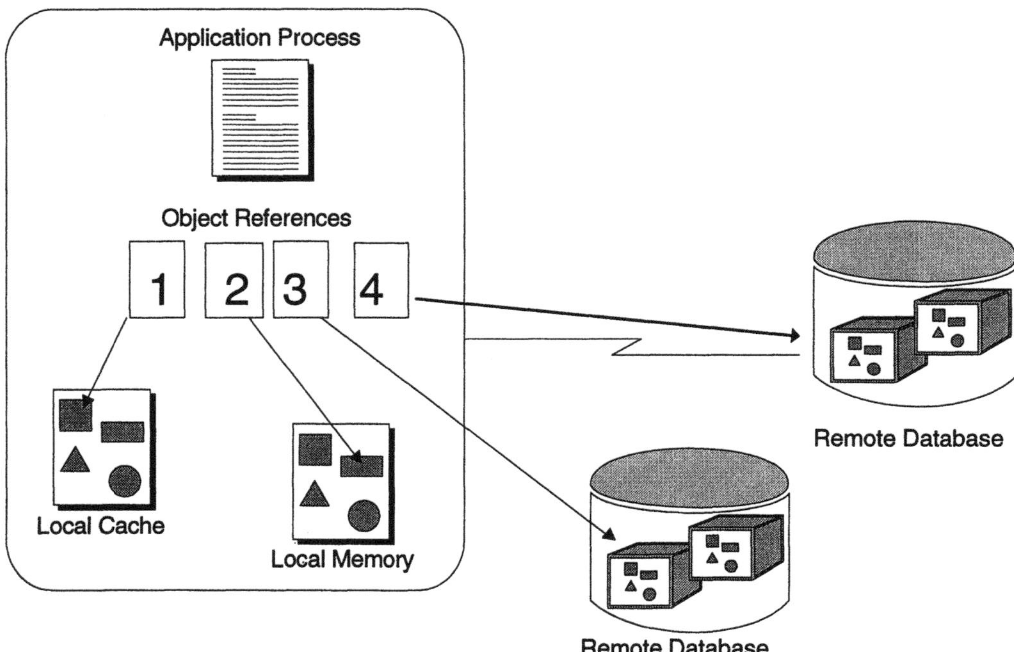


At the lowest level, ODB accesses persistent objects through 64-bit object identifiers (OIDs). Each object in an ODB federated database has a unique OID that does not change for the lifetime of the object. OIDs allow ODB to locate and manage objects with flexibility and a modicum of safety.

The product allows concurrent access to an object database by multiple users and processes on a network. ODB ensures databases in a federation remain consistent when multiple processes concurrently access a database. It provides concurrency control through locking, transaction semantics, and for C++ applications, the ability to simultaneously support multiple readers and one writer on the same container.

ODB is a multiprocessing system, allowing simultaneous multiple access to objects. To ensure consistency, object database access is restricted through the use of locks. A process can obtain either a read lock – which allows other processes to read the objects – or an update lock – which prevents all other processes from reading or modifying the objects. A process can also obtain shared and exclusive locks that support propagation across composite objects.

The product supports locking at arbitrary levels of granularity. Granularity can be determined using the flexible storage hierarchy provided for this purpose.

Locks are granted automatically and transparently to an application. Users also can explicitly set locks. For each collaborated database in which resources are pooled, known as federated databases, locks are managed by a lock server. For non-partitioned federated databases, the lock server is a centralized resource; there is one lock server running per federated database. All applications accessing the federated database request a lock for objects from this lock server. For partitioned federated databases, there is one lock server per partition.

Object database applications perform work on objects within a transaction. Transactions allow a collection of operations to appear as a single automatic operation to the object database. Either all of the operations are performed or none are completed. Once a transaction is applied to the object database, the changes made to objects during the transaction are stored on disk. However, an application may choose to abort a transaction at any time up to the commit point, leaving the object database in its original state.

Users can checkpoint changes made during a transaction. The checkpoint stores changes to the object database, allowing other applications to access the changes. However, the transaction remains active and all previously set locks are still held by the application.

ODB provides a check-out/check-in mechanism allowing users to lock a container or database for an extended period of time, rather than for a single session. This option is useful for large design projects which must isolate and work on a piece of a large design.

With ODB, an application can create separate versions of an object and track its version genealogy over time. This feature is essential for applications that perform design and configuration management of complex systems. The application can perform linear and branch versioning of objects, and can specify a particular version as the default version.

ObjectStore and ODB are but two of the full-fledged OODBMS offerings available to system developers and technology managers. As with all such products, their sales are increasing steadily, but they still have not achieved the massive breakthrough forecast by some pundits.

One of the fundamental reasons for this slower-than-expected acceptance is the enormous investment users have made in RDBMS. Shifting from an entrenched RDBMS to a technically challenging OODBMS can be a wrenching experience. The old adage "If it works, do not fix it" is entirely applicable in this situation.

## Technical Issues

There is an endless array of technical issues associated with OODBMS technology. What follows is a distillation of these issues into the most critical elements affecting object database operation.

As with any data resource, an OODBMS must offer integrity and reliability. Data integrity is essential to avoid the high cost of data corruption. Referential integrity must also be maintained, which means deleting the relationship between two objects when one of the objects is deleted. Failure recovery is another aspect vital to mission-critical applications. Recovery from failure must occur as quickly as possible.

The object model is another important issue. This category concerns requirements relating to the complexity and size of data. Specific requirements include:

- *Large Objects* – The application requires object sizes larger than 10 KB

- *Small Objects* – The application requires object sizes less then 150 bytes

- *Complex Relationships* – The application requires a network of objects with many-to-many relationships, for example, what parts go with what car

- *Complex Objects* – The application must store variable length data

- *Composite Objects* – The application must store hierarchies of components

- *Flexible Structure* – The application must store data whose underlying structure can be altered

Transactional activity is concerned with user data access. Some of the techniques are:

- *Multiple Readers per Object* – Many users need to simultaneously read the same data. Less than 10 is low, 10 to 150 is medium, and anything beyond 150 is high

- *Many Updaters per Object* – Many users must simultaneously update the same data. Less than five is low, five to 25 is medium, and anything beyond 25 is high

- *Length of Ownership* – This occurs when a user establishes ownership of an object for an extended duration, even beyond the termination of a process. Meanwhile, a short ownership duration implies no such transaction survives after the termination of a process.

Database distribution is concerned with the application's network configuration and to what degree the data is distributed. Some of the requirements are:

- *Many Users* – Multiple user processes must connect to a database at any one time. Less than 100 is low, 100 to 750 is medium, and anything beyond 750 is high.

- *Many Databases* – Users must access data in many databases. Less than four is low, four to 25 is medium, and anything beyond 25 is high

- *Many Sites* – Users and databases at many sites interact with one another. Less than four sites is low, four to 15 is medium, and anything beyond 15 is high

---

- *Heterogeneous Systems* – Users have to access data stored in different data formats among non-homogeneous configurations

Performance is a critical yardstick when evaluating a database. Some of the factors impacting performance are:

- *Scalability* – Are additional resources easily added to either maintain or improve performance? Maintaining consistent performance is very important

- *Traversal* – Applications demand immediate response time when migrating from one object to another as a result of a relationship between them

- *Updating Objects* – Applications require prompt response time when updating an object

- *Execution Time* – Complex methods associated with an application must execute quickly

The application's operating environment has a measurable impact on system efficiency. Among the issues are:

- *Language Support* – If the application is of a type that benefits from C++ or Smalltalk support, that application must be developed in one of those languages

- *Standards Support* – Database standards compliance such as ODMG-93 is important to the long-term viability of the application

- *Legacy Support* – The ability to interface to older, established systems is always an important consideration

## Future Trends

In terms of marketplace acceptance, OODBMS products will continue to broaden their heretofore narrow application base by linking to existing technologies such as RDBMS entities. Adherence to industry standards is another method by which object vendors of all types hope to widen their appeal. Examples of these standards include ODMG-93, SQL, CORBA, ANSI X3H7 (group working to consolidate or map differing object models), ANSI X3J12 (C++ standards committee), and Microsoft's ODBC. The ODMG standard (ODMG-93) is the specification most directly managing OODBMS issues.

The ODMG was organized in the early 1990s. It consisted of object database vendors such as Object Design, Inc., Objectivity, Inc., Versant, Ontos, and other technology participants. The object model and programming language bindings developed for the ODMG-93 standard were closely related to existing industry practices. ODMG's goal was to coalesce and specify ongoing technology, not to reinvent the wheel.

All founding members of the ODMG were also members of the OMG Special Interest Group on Object Databases. In the OMG Object Model shown in Figure 4.7, ODMG-93 is a profile. In OMG terms, a profile is a set of components that meet the requirements of particular product categories.

## Figure 4.7 Object Management Group Components and Profiles

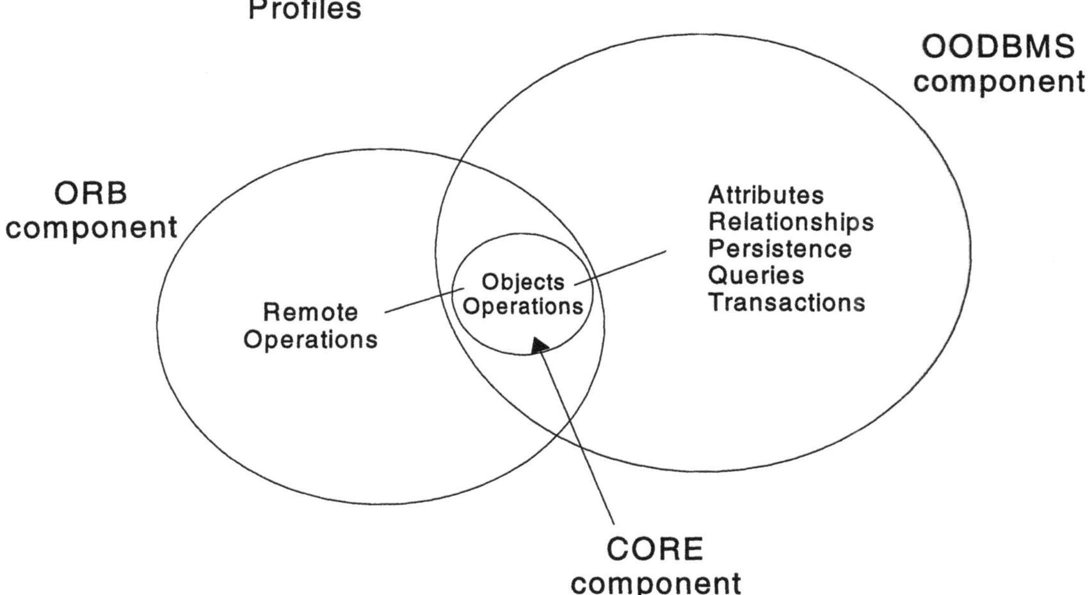


The OODBMS profile includes the Core Component, which defines objects and operations on objects. The profile also adds relationships between objects and persistent objects, in addition to attributes of objects, queries, and transactions. ODMG-93 is the formal specification of this profile.

The standard itself consists of an object model and a set of programming language bindings. ODMG-93 Version 1.2 includes the C++ language binding. The model specifies precisely how information is structured in the database. Issues covered include objects and their attributes, relationships between objects, and operations on objects. The programming language bindings map those concepts into Smalltalk and C++. C++ serves as an application programming interface (API) so a developer can perform additions, deletions, and updates on the objects stored in a database.

The basic tenets of the object model are as follows:

- The basic model entity is the object

- Objects are divided into types; all objects of the same type display common characteristics

- The behavior of the objects is defined by a set of operations that can be performed on them

- The state of objects is defined by the values they possess for a set of properties; these properties can be inherent attributes of the object or relationships between the object and one or more additional objects

- Object types are organized into subtype and supertype gradients. Subtypes inherit behavior and state from their supertypes

While ODMG-93 has been important to the expansion of OODBMS technology, SQL currently remains the most common database standard in use. SQL3, the latest version of the standard, offers promise of broad support for object extensions and makes it easier for OO applications to access SQL-compliant DBMS offerings. SQL also is a ready technology for non-object applications to use with an object database.

In concert with ODBC, standard SQL statements can access object database information from non-object applications. This ability helps preserve the investment made in traditional SQL-based tools as object technology is adapted for new applications.

SQL is used for database access by a variety of applications. Developers directly building applications with traditional languages often program with SQL as a database language that can be compiled and provide portability. Many 4GLs use SQL for a similar reason, but usually hide the details of the SQL language to simplify application development and to provide portability. Report writers and query tools rely on SQL for interoperability, meaning flexibility at runtime in accessing a variety of SQL-compliant databases. These uses of SQL are extremely common, and share an emphasis on portability and data independence.

As new applications are built using object technology and object databases are introduced into these environments, the ability to use these same traditional non-OO applications and tools to access information managed by the object database is important. For users with a significant investment in SQL, the ability to use standard SQL to access objects reduces their learning curve because they can treat the object database as simply another database.

When users access information in an object database using SQL, they can benefit from object technology without any additional investment. The application built with object technology and an object database can use its high performance and nontraditional functionality, while the SQL user can transparently access required textual or numeric information. Objects that contain information appropriate to an application can be accessed through standard SQL, with results returned to the application exactly as it would be by any other SQL-compliant data source.

SQL3 takes this a step further by providing object extensions within the context of SQL. SQL3 object extensions can be used for invoking methods, navigating between objects, and accessing nested data structures. SQL tools and applications will then have the flexibility of optionally utilizing object database-specific functions through the SQL interfaces.

Although using SQL for access to an object database is an important innovation, using SQL for access to non-relational database architectures is relatively common. Many network, hierarchical, inverted list, and other proprietary databases have offered SQL access by interpreting the semantics of SQL into the conceptual rules enforced by that particular database. Object database technology provides the same opportunity by mapping the semantics of tables, rows, and fields to object classes, objects, and data fields.

A complete mapping of SQL to an object database includes mapping the data definition language (DDL), used for defining tables, attributes, domains, and constraints, and the data manipulation language (DML) used for creating, querying, updating, and deleting data managed by the database. The DML portion of the language includes query and modification of data. For SQL, the most basic operations are Select, Insert, Delete, and Update. Mapping these to an object database first requires matching the context of the data involved, then the semantics of the operation. The SQL engine maps relational tables to object classes, rows to objects, row identifiers to object identifiers, and columns to object data members. Table and attribute information to identify accessible table and column names are also available through SQL operations.

In addition to standard SQL syntax, SQL3 includes object extensions for invoking object methods, navigating relationships between objects, and accessing nested structures. Extents and virtual object identifiers can also be supported. Table 4.5 illustrates SQL constructs relative to object technology.

## Table 4.5 SQL and Object Structures

| SQL Construct | Definition | Object Database Equivalent |
|---|---|---|
| Database | The scope of all stored data | Database |
| Table | A 2-D array of data values referred to as rows and columns. A specific data value belongs to exactly one row and one column. All data values are of identical types. All rows have values for all columns. | Object class |
| Column | One unit of the vertical dimension of a table. All data values in a column have the same data attribute. A single column is associated with all rows in a table. | An object's data member. Field types include SQL supported filed types and embedded structures and dynamic arrays. |
| Row | One unit of the horizontal dimension of a table. A row contains data volumes from each column in the table. All columns are considered to be in the same order for all rows. Rows are analogous to records and are the smallest unit of data in the table. | Object |
| Row ID | A unique reference to a single row entry. | Object identifier |
| Index | Defines the logical order of the rows of a table. A table may have one or more indexes, each defining a separate ordering. An index is internally maintained and used whenever an access is determined to be faster using the index than through sequential file search. | Index |

A process architecture for implementing an SQL to object database interface is shown in Figure 4.8. OO applications can submit requests directly to the object database client or server system, while ODBC-compliant applications transfer their requests to an SQL mapping process that converts the SQL constructs to appropriate object database requests. These are passed to the object database and results are passed back, using the same ODBC mechanisms.

## Figure 4.8 Process Architecture

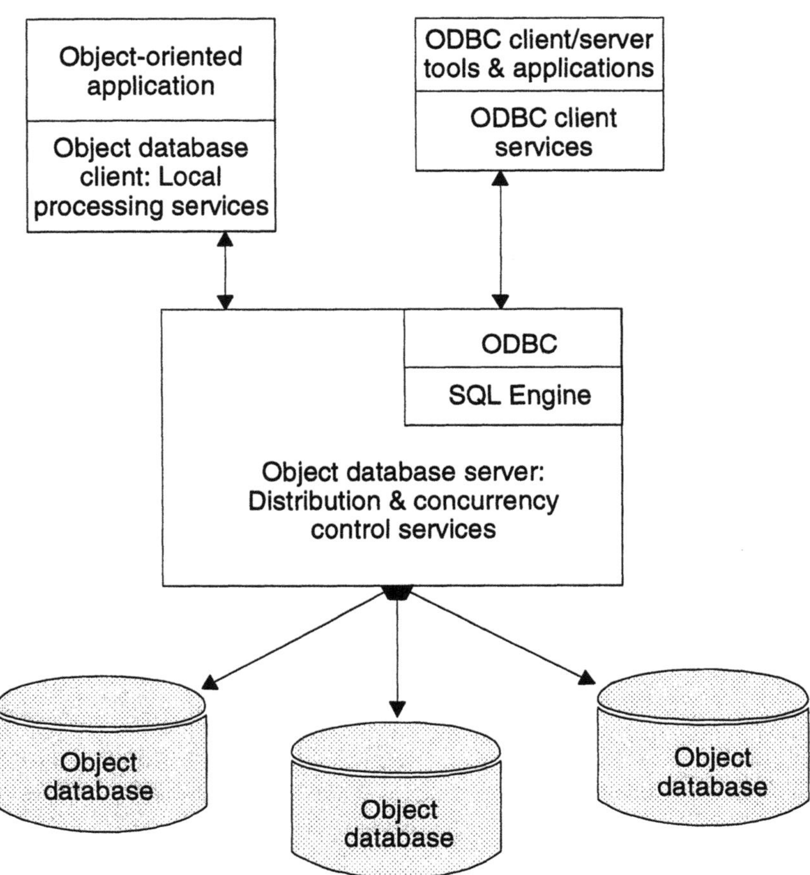

# Chapter 5

# Object-Oriented Programming Options

## Background and Benefits

There are two major groupings in the OO language competition One is advocated by the purists who state almost everything is an object. This group favors Smalltalk and its progeny.

The other grouping adopts a hybrid approach. Here, OO constructs are appended to a procedural language. The leading product in this category is C++. Another rising star in the hybrid grouping is OO COBOL.

In general, purist languages such as Smalltalk offer robust class libraries and an effective set of development tools. Hybrid entities such as C++ emphasize runtime speed and ease of adding OO extensions to the language. Both language types have a long learning curve in terms of efficient implementation.

Smalltalk usage has not quite kept pace with that of C++ in recent years. C++ gained great impetus from the popularity of its forebearer, C, in the early 1980s. By adding OO extensions to C, a ready-made constituency was assured for those intrepid pioneers migrating to object technology. It was much easier to adopt a language that many developers were already familiar with than to embark on a brand new programming experience with Smalltalk.

The chief benefit of OO programming languages, whether hybrid or otherwise, is their ability to model extremely complex, real-world entities.

Object orientation is a totally different experience for traditional programmers; a different mindset is required. Once learned, however, there is no question that object techniques are more in concert with the real world than that of the procedural methods.

Programming transforms from a code writing task to developing models using classes. OO programming generates fewer lines of code, simpler logic flows, and generally more understandable modules. These modules manifest a clear relationship between the conceptual model and the object model.

Once object technology acquires a degree of maturity in the organization, a repository of pre-defined class libraries is accumulated. This significantly reduces future development work because these objects and methods can be repeatedly reused. The property of inheritance encourages new object creation by supporting reuse of existing resources rather than rebuilding everything from the beginning.

OO languages also help developers by supporting modular program construction. Objects make it possible to keep data and the methods that act on that data together. Program maintenance is thus facilitated. In traditional language updates, there always is a concern that modifying one subroutine will have unanticipated impact elsewhere in a program or programs. Objects, on the other hand, are self-contained; they are encapsulated and there is no "domino effect" when change is imposed.

The largest single challenge facing object technology implementors is to acquire and retain skilled OO professionals. As has been often cited, the learning curve is quite steep – even for veteran programmers.

In the object arena, there are some skills that are high in demand and some that are declining. There is no problem identifying which programming talents are predominant: Smalltalk and C++ fit that bill. For the future, OO COBOL and Java will achieve a significant degree of support. Currently, however, C++ is the leading OO language, with Smalltalk coming in a close second.

## Functional Steps

Programming represents but one step on the path to object technology development. It is a very important step, but just one of many way stations on the road to object "nirvana." There have been several studies conducted focusing on early adopters of this technology. These studies have described lessons learned by companies such as Federal Express, IBM, and American Airlines.

Among these lessons, programming languages occupy only a small portion. There are numerous other issues that must be considered. It is useful to review these issues to place the consideration of programming languages in proper perspective. Many of these items represent common sense and are applicable to almost any human endeavor:

- *Educate management* – Object technology involves a paradigm shift. Do not expect executives to grasp it in a half-day seminar. Be prepared for organizational resistance and cultural barriers to new ways of thinking and working.

- *Recruit a high-level sponsor* – Secure executive sponsorship early-on from a sponsor, or champion, who is technologically literate or keenly interested in technology as a strategic asset

- *Set expectations appropriately* – Initial OOP projects are likely to be more difficult, expensive, and time-consuming than anticipated. Be conservative about short-term payback and emphasize that shortened delivery cycles will occur only after a solid base of experience has been established.

- *Learn from experienced peers* – This can include seeking out companies engaged in business-critical object technology projects, attending OO conferences that feature "user" speakers, and asking vendors and associations for introductions to object-experienced peers.

- *Recruit and carefully manage outside experts* – Identify vendors and consultants with successful track records in large-scale object technology implementation. Make sure the internal team owns the project and plan carefully for skills transfer.

- *Target developers based on personal motivation* – Personal curiosity and intellectual curiosity can be far more important than specific programming experience.

- *Work in small, geographically close teams* – Teams of about five people are ideal for the intensive communication OO development requires. Large teams should be divided into smaller sub-teams.

- *Plan for new roles and skills* – New roles can include facilitators who act as mentors and educators, object analysts and designers; architects responsible for the overall object model; librarians who keep track of class libraries; and assemblers who create applications from existing libraries of objects.

- *Target object-based projects wisely* – Appropriate targets can include small, business-critical applications; complex, interactive applications that can benefit from object modeling; families of closely related applications; and projects that require multiple or continuous rounds of user input.

- *Invest heavily in training* – OOP concepts present the greatest difficulty for newcomers. Learning new development environments and languages is a more moderate challenge by comparison. Strategic investment in training will pay off many times during development.

- *Recognize that analysis and design are difficult* – Qualified outside consulting help is essential for initial analysis and design. No single method is dominant; just pick one and stay with it. It can take a year or more to develop internal staff with expertise in this area.

- *Consider building an enterprise model* – An enterprise model simulates companywide business processes. Building an enterprise model can help a company identify common sets of objects and decide which ones to develop first.

- *Choose an OO language carefully* – Current languages have strengths and weaknesses. C++ is dominant, but many newcomers to objects have had better success starting with Smalltalk because of its pure approach and moving on to other more powerful languages once the concepts are clear.

- *Evolve prototypes into production systems* – OOP is well-suited to an iterative approach to application development. Developers can work side-by-side with users in an ongoing code-and-test process.

- *Conduct regular design and code reviews* – Regular reviews ensure appropriate modeling and consistency among classes. Because team members stay better informed about each other's activities, regular reviews also encourage code reuse.

- *Focus early on performance* – Object programmers can and should focus on performance at every step of the development process. It should not be left to last-minute adjustments.

- *Position reuse as a long-term benefit* – Short-term benefits of OOP include increased flexibility, lower maintenance, and business-modeling capabilities. Analysis and design reuse come later, and code reuse is not likely until a company has completed at least two or three large-scale projects.

- *Put organization structures in place* – Reuse cannot occur unless some form of library is accessible, well-promoted, and easy-to-use, with appropriate assistance available as necessary.

- *Create new incentives* – Programmers should be encouraged to create and use reuse code, not to write or rewrite large quantities of code.

- *Develop OO metrics* – These can include predictive metrics such as time required, resources required, risk of failure, and business impact; structural metrics such as the number and size of classes; and productivity metrics such as costs, team size, and reuse achieved.

## C++

C++ is an OO version of the original C language. Unlike Smalltalk, which is a pure language, this hybrid has instilled some compromises to insure fast execution and small code size.

C++ is a superset of C and thus compatible with its ancestor. Existing C code can be incorporated into C++ programs. C++ uses compile-time binding and the specific class of an object – the most general class an object can belong to must be specified by the programmer. This specification minimizes code size and enhances run-time efficiency, but relinquishes some of the capability to reuse classes.

One of the earliest versions of C++ emanated from Bell Laboratories in the early 1980s. At that time, it had no programming tools, no debuggers, and certainly no pre-existing class libraries.

In those early days, Smalltalk was available, but was deficient in its ability to communicate with the outside world. Objective C (another C language extension from Stepstone) was technically similar to C++, but lacked the clout of a Bell Labs relationship. Thus, C++ emerged as the dominant language.

The initial C++ user base was minuscule and almost entirely UNIX-related. There were no templates or runtime data available. Only single inheritance was supported. Despite these limitations, early implementors were optimistic because they envisioned large libraries of reusable code emerging as the language gained acceptance. As with so many advances in the world of technology, current reality has not come close to matching early promise.

C++ is a hybrid language with strong typing, stronger in fact than C. It now supports single and multiple inheritance and provides limited support of dynamic binding through the use of virtual functions. Memory allocation and release are explicitly performed within the program. There are no language constructs to support data persistence, although the stream I/O facilities can be used for very simple file I/O. C++ does not support the treatment of classes as objects.

C++ is used widely, particularly for large-scale projects. The biggest advantages of C++ are the wide range of product and vendor support and the growing pool of expertise available. There are a large number of compilers and development environments available across a range of hardware platforms and operating systems, and most OO databases support direct access from C++. Many of the application development tools also support linkage to C++ routines.

C++ is a complex language to learn from scratch. For programmers who have previous experience with C, there are sometimes difficulties in writing code in a truly OO manner; there is a school of thought that says such programmers should be taught Smalltalk before switching from C to C++. The complexity and the lack of enforcement of OO concepts means systems can be poorly implemented in C++ unless there are strong management and review procedures associated with the project.

There is no formal base class library defined for C++, but there are a number of commercial class libraries providing some basic classes (for example, list handling). C++ is the only object language with a significant number of suppliers providing independent class libraries.

C++ is not the perfect OO language, but it is likely to be the first choice for systems developed by more than one person or running on a more powerful machine than a PC.

There are a variety of C++ compilers available, mostly tailored to one particular platform. Regarding UNIX, the hardware vendors usually sell compilers such as Sun and Digital, for example. For OS/2, IBM supplies the C Set++ compile and development environment, while Borland sells a version of their compiler. Concerning Microsoft Windows, compilers are available from Microsoft and several others.

Developers do not just buy a C++ compiler anymore. In the Windows world in particular, one acquires an environment, not just a compiler. The compiler itself is only one element in a coordinated aggregation of tools that may include a browser, text editor, debugger, and an assortment of supporting development aids.

Some of the products in this arena include Borland's C++, Symantec's C++ 7.x, and Microsoft's Visual C++ 4.x. These and other C++ compilers for the Windows market have their strengths and weaknesses, but the Microsoft offering has achieved widespread distribution. This fact does not necessarily mean it is the best product, however, just the most visible.

Visual C++ features a robust, tightly integrated development environment (IDE). Its Component Gallery object repository provides software reuse and management. To place a class into an application, for example, a developer acquires a copy of it from the Component Gallery and places it in the application.

Visual C++ offers just-in-time (JIT) debugging. When running a debug release of an application, any runtime error causes the system to react immediately before there is a crash. The system then displays a dialogue box that presents the choice of either terminating the application or transferring to the debugger.

One of the potential problems with Visual C++ is its intensely robust functionality. While a strength on one hand, it can be easy to lose one's place in this labarynthian model. Another area of concern is its complete adherence to 32-bit processing. Older systems such as Windows 3.1 and 3.11, which execute on 16-bit platforms, must use a different version of the compiler. Visual C++ 4.x is strictly targeted to Windows 95, NT, and Win32 platforms.

One of the components bundled with Visual C++ is data access objects (DAO). DAO consists of objects that comprise the programmer's interface to Microsoft's Jet component (or engine) as depicted in Figure 5.1. This Jet engine serves as a database manager for Visual Basic and Access. DAO is implemented as a COM-compliant library and works in 32-bit Windows environments. It gives quick access through Jet to native Access data using identical abstract data objects found in Visual Basic.

## Figure 5.1 Data Access from Visual C++ 4.0

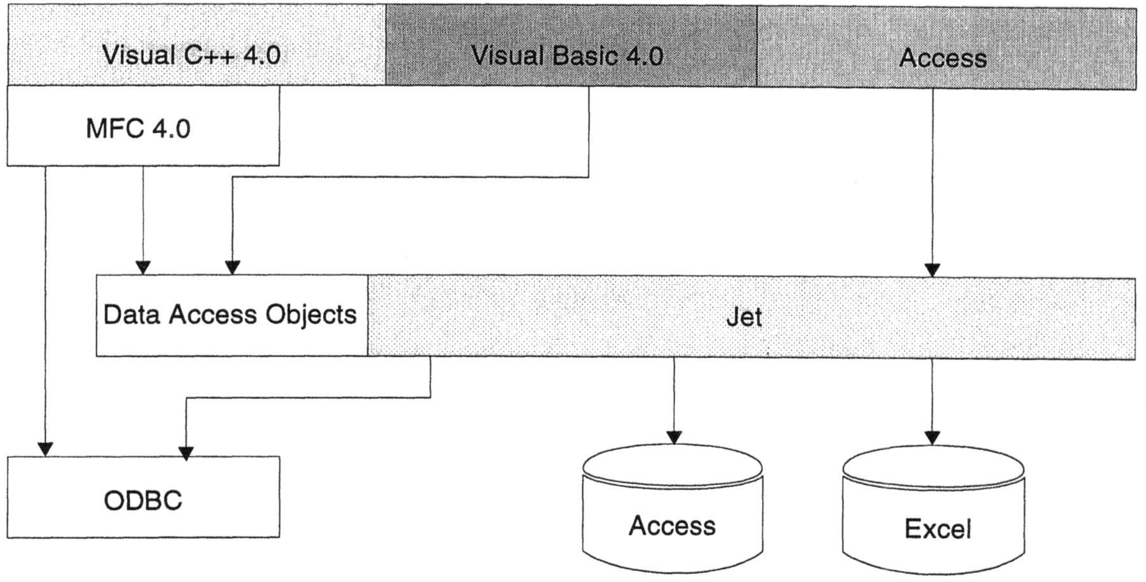


**Data access from Visual C++ 4.0**

Microsoft Foundation Classes (MFC) Version 4.0 is included in Visual C++. It encapsulates DAO objects into C++ classes, which are similar in structure to those that encompass ODBC. This encapsulation provides MFC developers a consistent path to both technologies.

C++ in all its variations is currently in the ascendancy. Languages such as Java will challenge its success as time passes because there are numerous flaws in C++ as an OO development language. Among them:

- The language does not provide a clear division between the interface to a class and the implementation of that class

- Evolution of the language has been uneven and continues to be so. Complexity has risen as new features have been added. Examples of the features are multiple inheritance and templates. Desirable features all but glacially slow in the pace of their addition to the language

Additional factors causing escalating complexity within the specification are a half-dozen varieties of multiple inheritance, abstract classes, and a seemingly endless array of non-standard extensions.

## Smalltalk

Where C++ institutes some compromises to improve execution time and code size, Smalltalk invokes an aggressive approach. It is a pure OO language. Smalltalk uses runtime binding, unlike C++ compile-time binding. Nothing about the type of an object need be known before a Smalltalk program is run.

Smalltalk programs are generally developed in a much shorter time frame than C++ programs. One of the prime reasons for this is Smalltalk's extensive class library, which can be efficiently reused via inheritance.

Smalltalk's dynamic development environment is another positive factor. It is not explicitly compiled as C++, which makes the development process more flexible so optional scenarios can be tried, and class definitions quickly refined.

There is widespread consensus that Smalltalk, because of its pure "objectness," takes longer to master than C++. Most of the extra time is spent learning OO methods and techniques, rather than specifics of a particular programming language. In fact, Smalltalk is simpler from a syntax standpoint than C++.

Early versions were produced in the 1980s by ParcPlace Systems, Digitalk, IBM, and a few others. ParcPlace and Digitalk have since merged into one company.

Smalltalk consists of a set of classes and a runtime environment. The classes themselves provide a development environment the user can tailor through class adaptation. Until recently, Smalltalk only ran as a complete environment. A Smalltalk system included an OS and was the only program running on the machine. Implementations that work in a multitasking or windowed environment under UNIX, OS/2, Microsoft Windows, and Mac System 7 are now available.

Smalltalk is a pure language and is effectively untyped, as everything within Smalltalk is an object. It fully supports dynamic binding and only supports single inheritance. Storage allocation and deallocation are automated and Smalltalk performs automatic garbage collection to efficiently reutilize memory.

Smalltalk implementations are generally regarded as interpreters, but performance has been improved by techniques such as dynamic translation. Dynamic translation compiles a complete method before it is run and maintains a cache of recently executed methods in compiled format.

The original development of Smalltalk was for use as a research tool. The early implementations had the drawbacks of such a development. As a result, Smalltalk is still only supported by a small number of vendors and there is a smaller pool of expertise than for C++. It was designed for system development to be performed by a single individual, and tools for shared development are relatively new. However, interest in the language is increasing and HP has promoted a distributed version of Smalltalk that is CORBA-compliant. Screen-based development environments such as ParcPlace Systems' VisualWorks and IBM's VisualAge are also available to make user interface design and implementation simpler.

The advantages of Smalltalk: It is a pure language with a simple syntax and provides a very comprehensive and well thought-out development environment for small systems with a full standard class library. It is an excellent language for teaching the principles of object orientation. It is worth considering for small developments and is now sufficiently well supported to be a viable choice for larger projects.

Whatever the conventional wisdom about Smalltalk, one fact is clear. It is growing in acceptance and has become a popular application development language. In 1995, revenue from sales of Smalltalk tools jumped 60% from the year before. The C++ tools market is upwards of six times larger than that of Smalltalk, but Smalltalk's portability and productivity has produced limitations for Smalltalk innovation.

Smalltalk development environments are emerging at a steady pace. Among the most popular environments are Visual Smalltalk Enterprise and

VisualWorks from ParcPlace and Digitalk. These two companies have recently merged and will undoubtedly feature just one product at some point, but they presently maintain both offerings. Other products receiving strong support are VisualAge Team from IBM and Object Studio from VMark Software. Easel Corp. owned Object Studio until it was sold to VMark in 1995. Table 5.1 outlines some of the primary features of these development environments.

## Table 5.1 Smalltalk Development Environments

■ = Yes  ❑ = No

| | Object Studio 4.1 | VisualAge Team for Smalltalk 2.0 | Visual Smalltalk Enterprise 3.0 | VisualWorks 2.0 |
|---|---|---|---|---|
| **Development Platforms** | | | | |
| Windows 3.1 | ■ | ■ | ■ | ■ |
| Windows for Workgroups 3.11 | ■ | ■ | ■ | ■ |
| Windows NT 3.51 | ❑ | ❑ | ■ | ■ |
| Windows 95 | ❑ | ❑ | ❑ | ❑ |
| OS/23.0 | ■ | ■ | ■ | ■ |
| Mac System 7.01 or later | ❑ | ❑ | ❑ | ■ |
| Solaris 2.3 or later | ■ | ❑ | ❑ | ■ |
| AIX 3.25 or later | ■ | ❑ | ❑ | ■ |
| HP-UX 9.05 or later | ■ | ❑ | ❑ | ■ |
| **Relational Database Connectivity** | | | | |
| Sybase 10 (Sybase, Inc.) | Native | ODBC[1] | ODBC | Native |
| Microsoft SQL Server 4.21 (Microsoft Corp.) | Native | ODBC | ODBC | None |
| Oracle7 (Oracle Corp.) | Native | ODBC | ODBC | Native |
| DB2/2, Version 1.2 (IBM) | Native | ODBC/Native | ODBC | Native |
| SQLBase 5.11 (Gupta Corp.) | Native | ODBC | None | None |
| Rdb, Version 6 (Digital Equipment Corp.) | Native[2] | None | None | None |
| Informix 5.0 (Informix Software, Inc.) | Native[3] | ODBC | None | None |
| **Object Export Tools** | | | | |
| Versant 4.0 (Versant Object Technology) | ❑ | ❑ | ❑ | ■ |
| Object Store (Object Design, Inc.) | ❑ | ❑ | ❑ | ■ |
| Gemstone (Gemstone Systems, Inc.) | ❑ | ❑ | ■ | ■ |
| ODBMS 3.0 (VCSoftware) | ❑ | ❑ | ■ | ■ |
| Tensegrity 2.0 (Polymorphic Software, Inc.) | ❑ | ❑ | ■ | ■ |
| **Object Exchange Standards** | | | | |
| System Object Model (IBM) | ❑ | ■ | ■ | ■ |
| Distributed Computing Environment | ❑ | Third-party | ❑ | ❑ |
| OLE (Microsoft) | ■[4] | ❑ | ❑ | ■[5] |

1. Open Database Connectivity, 2. Relational database running on Windows platform only, 3. Informix running on UNIX platform only, 4. OLE 1.0. 5. OLE 2.0

Visual Smalltalk Enterprise 3.x demonstrates impressive strength in reuse, portability, and visual programming. It is an amalgamation of two separate tools from an earlier era:

1.  Its Smalltalk-based OO environment.

2.  Digitalk's Parts Workbench.

The product has a strong array of visual programming tools, class creation mechanisms, and reusability features. ODBC is directly supported, whereas SQL requires some original coding. Smalltalk link libraries provide scalability and portability to multiple platforms.

VisualAge Team 2.x has stressed team development by integrating a version control system which handles project and configuration management tasks. Its visual programming support uses a simplified component assembly approach. Improved navigation tools and editors aid class library manipulation. VisualAge Team provides a strong browser capability, which facilitates code reusability.

Object Studio 4.x presents an effective set of visual programming tools and a comprehensive aggregate of browsers. Small class library and weak team development facilities hold this product back somewhat. The product relies on developers to coordinate and manually manage their own version control mechanism – a virtual disaster.

Whether it be Smalltalk or C++, each language has unique capabilities. C++ has a massive syntax and precise data typing. Smalltalk, on the other hand, has minimal syntax and simple object manipulation features. Smalltalk adherents prefer the large, robust development environment. C++ proponents argue for its greater adaptability and freedom from environmental dependencies.

In the final analysis, there is no "better" language. The nature of the application provides the final determinant.

## Standards

There are numerous standards efforts in the object world in general. On the object programming language front, attention is focused on the work of ANSI Committee X3J12, which has been working on the C++ standard.

Although the C++ standard specification has stabilized, some vendors continue to add extensions or "value," as they like to call it. This addition results in non-standard implementations which restarts the whole cycle.

## Future Trends

Unlike procedural programming, which emphasizes algorithms and procedures, OOP emphasizes the binding of data structures with the methods to operate on the data. The idea is to design object classes that correspond to the essential features of a problem. Rather than fitting a problem to the procedural approach of a computer language, OOP allows the programmer to use the language to effectively model and solve real-world problems. A drawing program, for example, might define classes that represent rectangles, polygons, and circles. The class definitions would include the same functionality for each class such as move and rotate. A developer would then proceed to design a program by deriving subclasses and overriding existing methods or implementing new methods within each class.

This development approach allows developers to divide problems into small, manageable modules of code, where the principle of encapsulation insulates developers from knowing the implementation details. Due to the principle of inheritance, developers can subclass to derive new classes from existing ones and be provided with the ability to add extensions.

In addition, polymorphism provides the developer flexibility to create multiple definitions for functions, which allows classes to be more general and, hence, more reusable. It also allows new components and functions to be added easily and without disturbing the existing system. Implementing OOP makes it possible to design more extensible, reusable, and maintainable software.

By helping developers more productively design and produce code, the advantages of OOP have proven to be a significant advance over traditional programming techniques. However, though the programming job is made easier as the developer works at a higher level of abstraction with objects and class libraries, the developer must still assemble the pieces into a cohesive whole. Simply changing from procedural techniques to OOP does not rectify the problem. Developers are responsible for providing infrastructure and are not provided with a clean mechanism for extending functionality. Even with OOP, developers write code because they are still responsible for providing the flow of control of the application. Frameworks further carry the OOP paradigm by providing infrastructure and flexibility for deploying OOT.

Although frameworks are not new to the software industry, there is a great deal of discussion about them in object technology circles. What exactly are frameworks? A widely accepted definition states: "A framework is an aggregation of classes that embodies an abstract design for solutions to a family of associated problems."

Another way of regarding frameworks is as a prefabricated structure or template of a working program. For example, an application framework provides the support and "default" behavior for drawing windows, scroll bars, and menus.

Frameworks may be the most important advancement in OOT because they provide an infrastructure and flexible interfaces, and they avoid the problems and overhead traditional programming imposes on developers. With well-designed frameworks, it is easier to add extensions, factor out common functionality, enable interoperability, and improve software maintenance and reliability.

The way frameworks, in general, achieve these benefits over other development approaches is based on two fundamental principles:

1. Frameworks provide infrastructure and design. They are not just collections of classes. Rather, frameworks come with rich functionality and "wired-in" interconnections between the object classes that provide an infrastructure for the developer. These inter-connections provide the architectural model and designs for developers and free them to apply their expertise on the problem domain. By providing an infrastructure, the framework decreases the amount of standard code the developer must program, test, and debug (see Figure 5.2).

2.  The framework does the calling, as framework-oriented programming requires a new way of thinking. In procedural systems, the developer's own program provides all of the structure and flow of execution and makes calls to function libraries as necessary. However, in framework-oriented programming, the roles are reversed. The role of the framework is to provide the flow of control, while the developer's code waits for the call from the framework. This is a significant benefit because developers need not be concerned with details, but can focus their attention on their particular problem domain.

However, this switch in control can be a significant change for developers experienced only in procedural programming. The developer must learn to think in terms of the responsibilities of the objects — what the objects are required to do — and let the framework determine when the objects should do it. Once the investment has been made to understand frameworks, developers will begin to realize the advantages framework-oriented programming can deliver over other development approaches.

## Figure 5.2 Frameworks

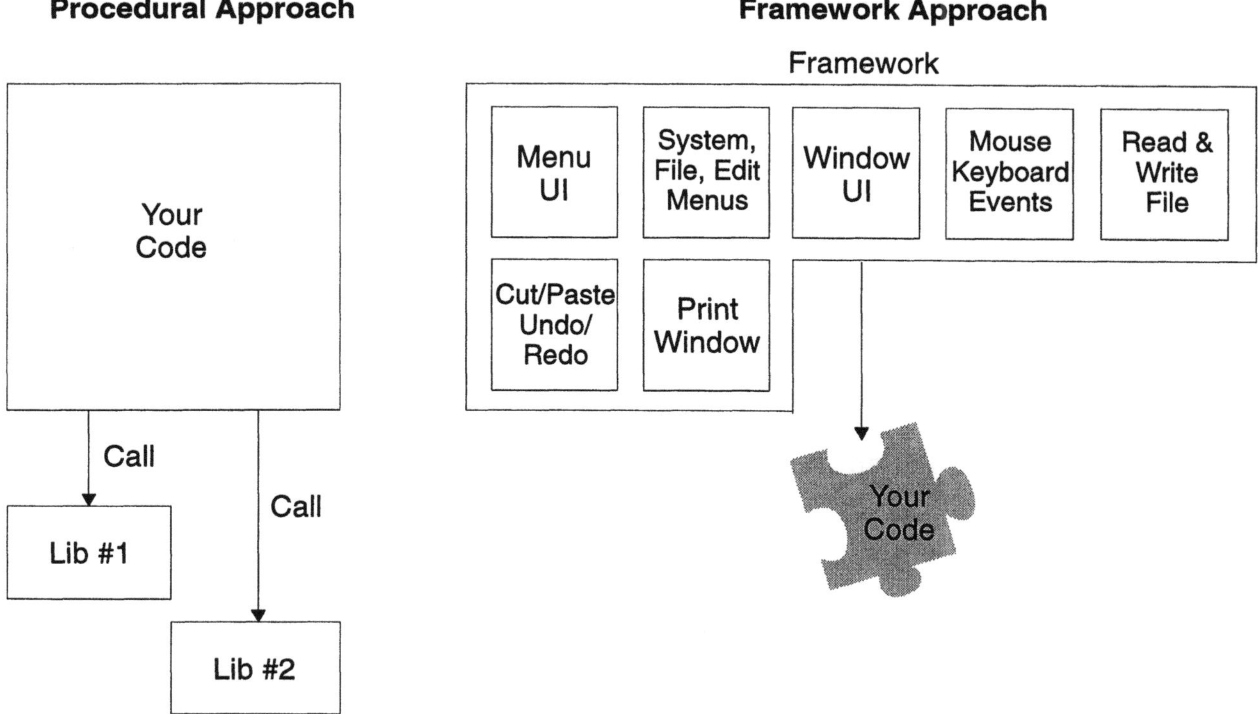

There are many types of frameworks (not all OO) on the market for solving various types of problems. The types of frameworks range from application frameworks that assist in developing the user interface, to lower-level frameworks that provide basic system software services such as communication, printing, and file systems support. Within this range, there also are domain-specific frameworks that address problems in particular areas. There are a number of commercially available application frameworks such as MacApp (Apple Computer). There are fewer system-level frameworks, but examples are multiplying steadily.

The overall benefit of frameworks: They enable a higher level of code and design reuse than what is practical with other design approaches. In addition to frameworks, there are other reuse technologies such as 4GLs, code generators, and class libraries. However, 4GLs and code generators are based on procedural programming techniques and cannot easily provide the infrastructure and design guidance possible from frameworks. While class libraries do improve code reuse, they provide functionality at a very low level and force the developer to provide the interconnections between the libraries.

The developer should realize the benefits from frameworks and reuse are gained over time because the productivity gains do not come just from the first or second use, but from multiple uses of the technology. There are several benefits to using frameworks, but this list summarizes the major advantages:

- *Provide infrastructure and architectural guidance* – By virtue of the interconnections among the class libraries, much of the needed functionality already exists in the framework, thus reducing coding, testing, and debugging efforts. In addition, frameworks encourage better design in the code developers do write by providing an example to guide them to more effectively utilize object technology. Applications developed with frameworks tend to be smaller, more maintainable, and reusable.

- *Provide a mechanism for extending functionality* – While objects and object classes provide interfaces for extending functionality at a fine-grained level, frameworks provide this flexibility at a higher level. In this way, applications can be developed by using the framework as a starting point and writing smaller amounts of code to modify or extend the framework's behavior. These extensions can be added without sacrificing compatibility and interoperability because the interfaces are well-defined.

- *Reduce maintenance* – Because of inheritance, when a framework bug is corrected or a new feature is added, the benefits of those changes become available more quickly to the derived classes. In addition, changes are made only in one place, thus, the chance of introducing additional errors in the code is minimized.

Frameworks represent an important future step for object technology in general, and OOP in particular. It raises the level of abstraction for the entire object technology experience.

# Chapter 6

# User Interaction

## Background and Benefits

To the user, the benefits of contemporary GUIs center on the look-and-feel. Objects on the screen can be manipulated to control the behavior of the compiler. As software objects encapsulate data and methods into a single entity, so do the icons a user views and controls on the screen.

GUIs often result in applications resembling real-world activities rather than austere programming processes. The old character-based interfaces as manifested in early DOS certainly aligned themselves with the line-entry, programming process mode.

GUIs long ago introduced the notion of intuitive system manipulation. Some did this more successfully than others, with the Mac perhaps a leader in this regard. All GUIs, however, were an order of magnitude easier to use than their earlier character-based counterparts.

The ultimate benefit of GUIs is allowing the user to move about in an environment that is closer to real-world experience and less like a structured computer program. The user can invoke a function immediately. For example, when connecting to a remote communications module, all necessary tools are loaded after the user clicks on a communications object.

Navigating among programs and functions is managed in a variety of ways by different GUIs. The icons are graphic representations of system functions; they are manifestations of object functionality. Interaction among these objects is supported by some form of rapid context switching methodology.

Apple's Mac 7.x handles rapid program loading and switching by transferring data between programs with a cut and paste function (see Figure 6.1). OO systems link objects among applications. These links are full duplex; altering data elements can cause an accompanying graph or table to be updated. Similarly, modifying that same graph or table can cause the underlying data elements associated with it to be changed. In Figure 6.1, this is annotated as "live paste and copy."

**Figure 6.1 Macintosh Context Switching**

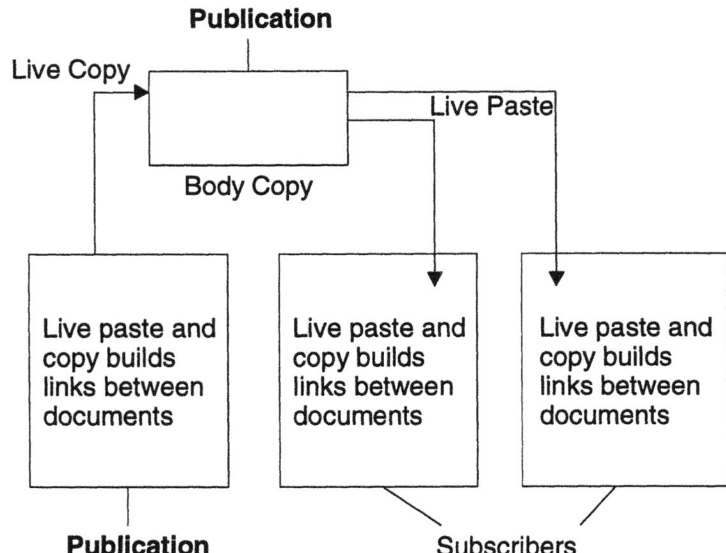


In the Mac environment, there is a publisher and subscriber element. Segments of documents can be copied (as in "cut") with a Publish command and placed in other documents with a Subscribe (as in "paste") command. The segments invoked by Publish are saved as separate documents with their own publication icons. Publishers and subscribers are sections of documents themselves. Subscribers receive notification when a publication is changed. A published element can appear in one or more subscribers.

To a developer, OO GUIs are a natural extension of object technology. The OO approach to user interface generation enables developers to improve the user interface mechanism by employing those attributes of modularity, reusability, and extensibility so closely aligned with object technology.

As GUI development capabilities have been refined in recent years, labor saving methodologies have been injected into the process. Frameworks have been introduced to improve the complexities of the programming task. Currently, universal frameworks comprised of abstract classes for each major user interface component have been built for most implementations of Windows and others.

## Graphical User Interfaces

The transition to a multimedia processing model is progressing at a rapid pace. Not all users require this resource-intensive set of services, but it is a valuable tool for those that do.

To build multimedia applications, programmers must contend with diverse types of data. OO interfaces and their underlying OS aid programmers in storing and accessing multimedia data. Because objects encapsulate both data and methods, displaying and/or editing a voice, video or graphic module reside within the domain of the object and its partner objects.

The power of OO tools and methods to manage complex aggregations of data such as is found in multimedia applications is vital to the success of this type of computing. GUIs that provide the user interface to multimedia functionality are built almost exclusively using object technology. Figure 6.2 depicts many of the steps involved in a user interface.

## Figure 6.2 User Interface Dialogue

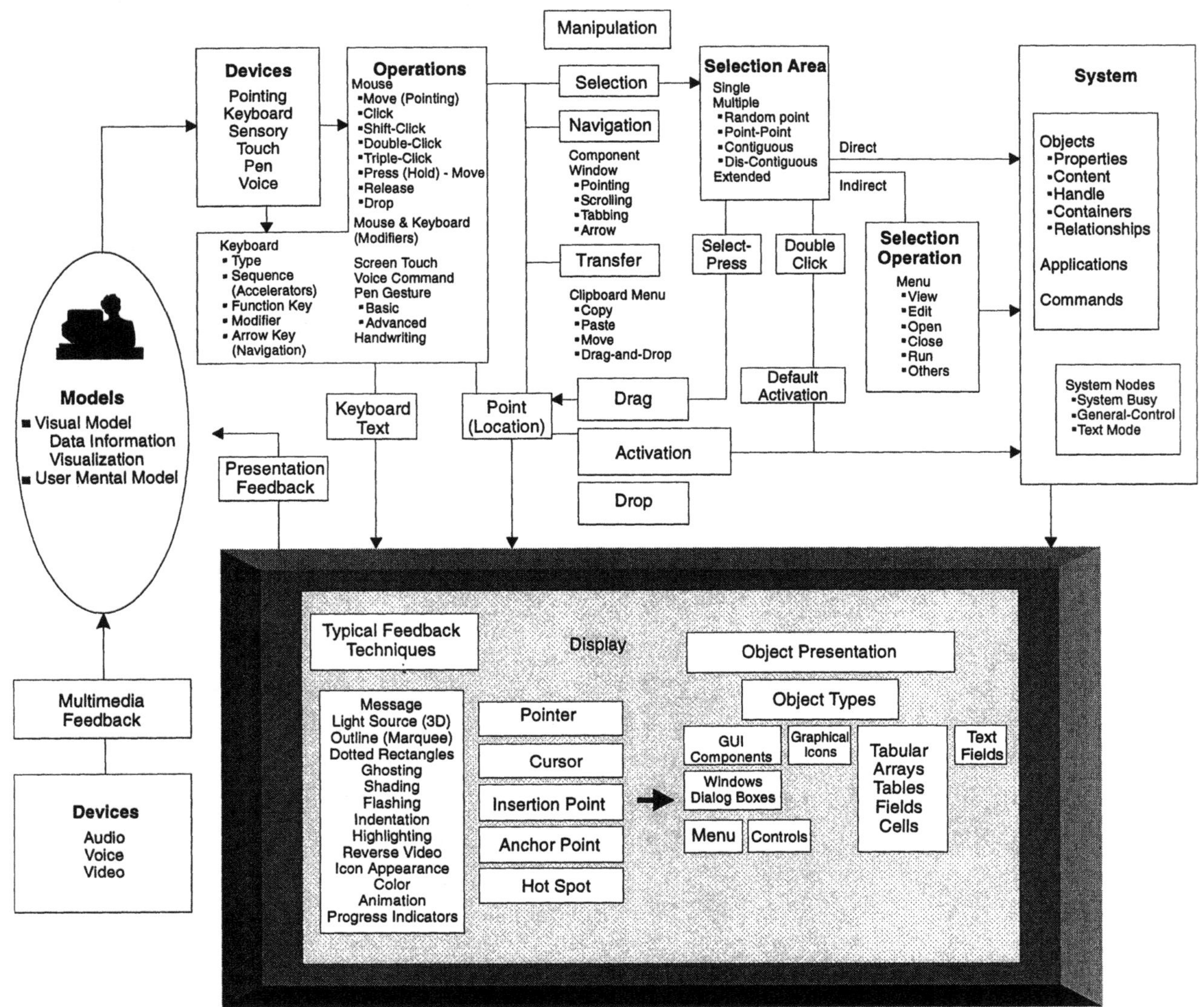


Major features of a contemporary user interface include:

- Multi-window display with dynamic window management

- Multimedia output

- Possible natural language interface

- 2-D and 3-D user interface devices

- SQL internal interface to non-text data

These commercial implementations all exhibit some of the qualities cited above. The examples discussed are not exhaustive; there are other equally credible manifestations in the marketplace. All of these interfaces continue to evolve and improve to meet the challenges of a changing technology.

Microsoft's strategic vision is to use the scalable architecture of the Windows OS to take advantage of varying hardware platforms. This will be achieved on two basic fronts:

1. Windows 95 will continue to exploit its relationship with Pentium processors, providing sufficient functionality for most desktop users. Windows' direct relationship with Intel processors has received widespread acceptance by the user community, and its 32-bit implementation supports preemptive multitasking.

2. Windows NT, a high-level implementation of the Windows model, is geared for advanced PC hardware, demanding desktop applications and server functions involved with C/S computing. While basic Windows is directed for use on Intel platforms, Windows NT is portable to other systems. It also offers multiprocessor operation, improved security, and a full 32-bit architecture and document-centric user interface defined by OLE.

Network operation in the Windows' environment is enhanced with features such as automatic network reconnection following failure and interfaces tuned for interoperation with all leading network operating systems. NT is designed specifically for network activity with high-speed drivers and a robust file system. It will support Microsoft's SQL Server and server applications from other vendors. NT also includes tools to help transition from OS/2 platforms. Microsoft's Windows Open Services Architecture (WOSA) provides interfaces to access data and services across heterogeneous computing environments.

IBM's Presentation Manager (PM) is the user interface to its OS/2 OS. It also is one of the primary sources for the popular Motif interface found in many UNIX environments. Like Windows, PM supports all popular interface devices, including pull-down menus, icons, pop-up dialogues, variable text fonts and sizes, a range of color implementations, and movable and overlapping window images.

PM is not just Windows on OS/2, however. Its graphical constructs adhere to IBM's Common User Access (CUA). Applications written in accordance with PM's API will be portable to systems embracing CUA guidelines. The three main components of the PM user interface are: Start Programs, Task Manager, and File System. All can be visible simultaneously in window images.

Start Programs allow users to initiate new processes by name from a menu. Task Manager allows users to switch among processes and sessions by mouse or hot-key operation. The File System portrays directories, file lists, and other features in graphical form. It also allows files to be copied, moved, deleted, printed or chosen for execution.

PM incorporates elements of object-orientation. It provides a view of objects as data, container, and device objects. PM makes excellent use of metaphors as proven by its support for new controls such as the container and notebook controls.

Motif is a distributed user interface that supports cooperative processing by using a C/S protocol. The implementation is comprised of two basic parts: Motif and X Window system. Motif itself is derived from technology created by IBM, Digital, and others.

Motif is based on X Windows and is endorsed by a large number of vendors. It includes an extensible user interface toolkit, a portable API, a user interface language, and a window manager. Motif's API specifies interfaces to the user interface toolkit and Motif resource manager. It is aligned with Windows and PM in terms of behavior and appearances. The API also supports tools to facilitate programmer productivity.

The user interface toolkit provides a standard GUI layer upon which applications are based. The toolkit also includes a graphic object library such as menus and scroll bars for use in building application user interfaces.

Motif's user interface language is an application development tool that supports user interface design and rapid prototyping. It enables an application developer to define and perfect the presentation characteristics of an application interface, regardless of the application code. This capability simplifies the description and maintenance of user interfaces.

Motif's window manager offers users a standard environment for manipulating application windows. It also allows users to modify windows by resizing or adding icons. In addition, the window manager implements procedures that determine where windows or icons can be situated and whether windows can overlap.

Motif has the same appearance and operating characteristics on a wide range of hardware platforms. From mainframes to midrange to the smallest system – Motif is consistent across all platforms. It also functions with a broad spectrum of OS implementations, including advanced interactive executive (AIX) and OSF/1.

Certainly in the UNIX environment – and to some degree with proprietary systems – Motif is the most universal implementation among GUI offerings. It stands a good chance of dominating its sector in the years ahead.

## Programming Tools for GUIs

The language of choice for basic GUI programming is C++. User interfaces, whatever their ultimate look-and-feel should be OO. An OO language should be used to manipulate the objects. Objects are a natural technique for representing components of a user interface and for managing their activity.

In terms of generic consistency, the X Window System which emerged from the UNIX world and is reflected in implementations such as Motif, serves as a good representation of GUI functionality. See where Motif fits into the GUI cycle in Figure 6.3.

## Figure 6.3 Graphical User Interface Genealogy

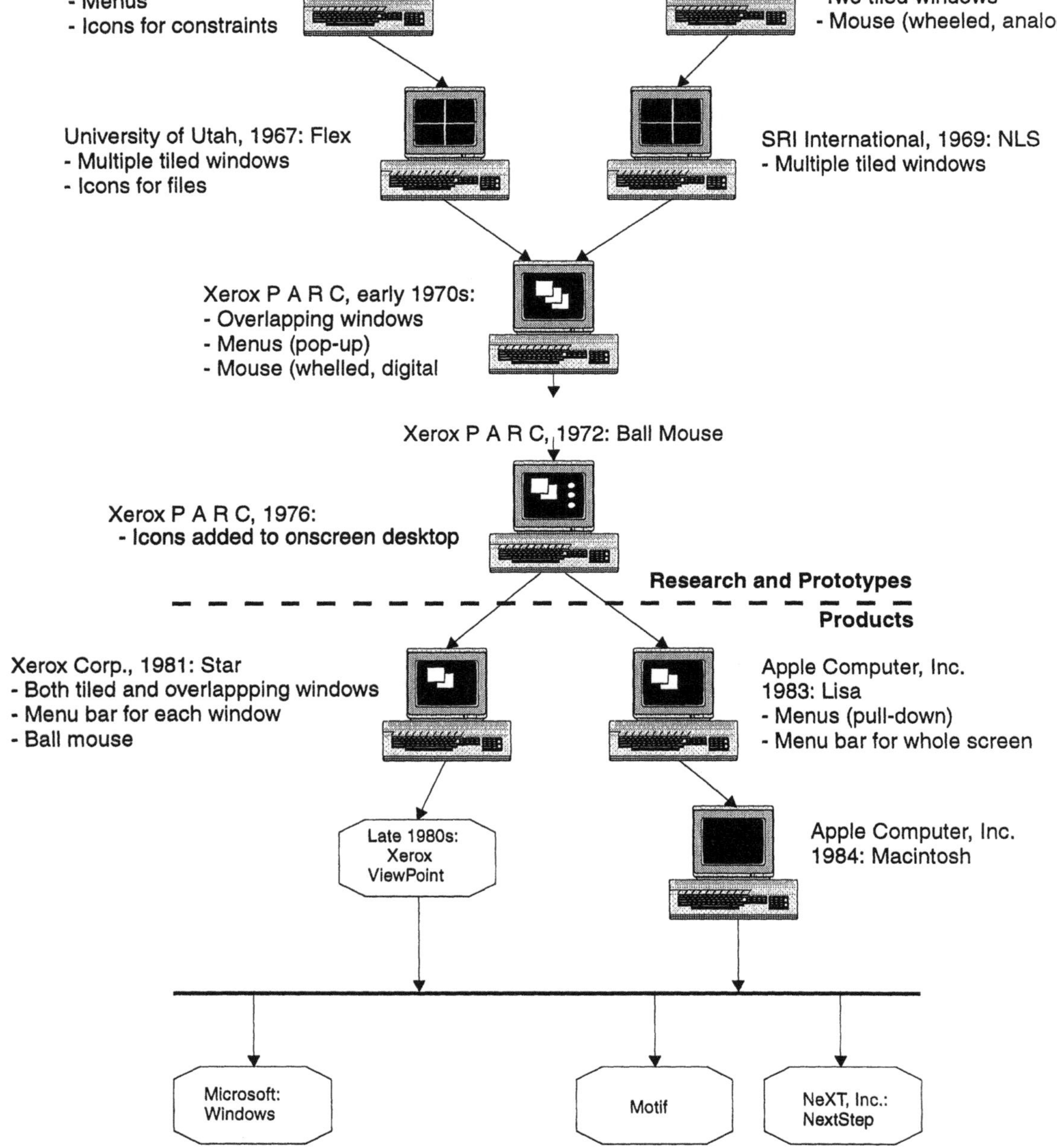


X Windows consists of four primary components: The X Server, Xlib, the Xtoolkit (XT), and the X protocol. X is an environment more concerned with providing a mechanism for GUIs than an actual look-and-feel. The actual look-and-feel is set by a combination of specialized toolkits and windows managers.

The architectural nomenclature of X Windows generally causes some confusion as the designated roles of client and server seem intuitively backward. The X Server runs on what most people would generally consider a client: The workstation. The X client, consisting of the Toolkit, the Xlib library of primitive graphics functions, and the actual application itself runs on what most people generally consider a server: A CPU node remote from the workstation that functions as an application server (see Figure 6.4).

## Figure 6.4 X Window Flow

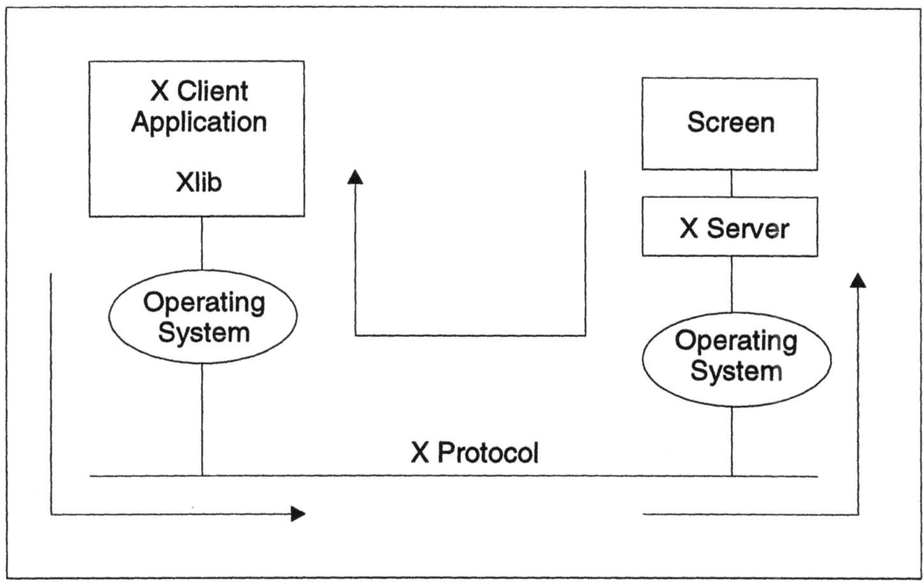


The X server is the program that runs on a workstation creating the basic interface and displaying graphics. The X Server is the intermediary between users and applications. It passes output from application clients to the display, and in turn passes user input to the application client for processing.

Xlib frees developers from worrying about the details of the X protocol. Originally, Xlib was a simple procedural interface to the X protocol. As X evolved, however, Xlib also grew to hold common utility routines.

Xlib is now a client-based library of graphics routines. The main function of Xlib and other layered libraries is to translate messages between client and server into X protocol requests.

The Xtoolkit consists of two parts: The intrinsics library and the widget set. Intrinsics are low-level user interface development tools and come standard with X. These are utility routines for implementing code and must work in conjunction with higher-level screen-based components called widgets. Together, these create the look-and-feel of the user interface.

Basically, widgets are specialized windows with I/O capabilities. They provide interface features such as scroll bars, dialog boxes, buttons, and fields. Applications can invoke these widgets within their own windows, thus freeing the developer from writing user interface code, while also creating a consistent look-and-feel across all supported applications.

The X protocol defines the data structures that transmit requests between applications and display servers over the network. Generally, these structures are created by Xlib or another layered library rather than by the application itself.

The X protocol is independent of OS, network transport or application language. The protocol only requires any error-corrected duplex byte stream with asynchronous operation (such as TCP/IP). Asynchronicity augments performance as it replaces the process of synchronous handshaking with pipelining. Exploiting this pipelining does require reliable transmission mechanisms, however. Should an application require synchronicity, however (such as a query for cursor position), X can wait for a response from the display server.

## Query Language Interface

The adoption of relational technology on a wide scale has led to the widespread use of non-procedural query languages as a method of accessing data, which provides a method for selecting sets of data fulfilling specified criteria. In relational terms, these were values derived from one or more tables, using table joins where appropriate. The result with an object approach will normally be a set of data attributes from the objects of a particular class that fulfill the specified criteria.

Providing such features presents a number of problems to OODBMSs. Principal among these features: The objects of a class may not be grouped together in the way that rows of a relational table are, and encapsulation means a method should run on each object of a class to verify whether it fulfills the criteria for inclusion in the query response.

Some OODBMS shield the developer from such problems by providing an SQL-like language for interrogating the database. This is frequently referred to as Object SQL. The ODMG defines standards for an OQL and most vendors conform to this standard. Products that already supply such a language are growing rapidly. A further issue is the ability to embed statements of such a language into a procedural language.

Another approach to supporting queries is through the use of sets of objects. These sets are normally objects and have supplied methods that allow querying of their members. This function provides a great degree of flexibility and allows the queries to be embedded in the normal language used for the system, but is not suitable for supporting end-user ad hoc querying of the database. Some OODBMS will automatically establish set objects for each class type defined within the database. This approach can be inefficient for large classes on which no querying is required. A better approach is to allow the developer to explicitly control the creation of a set object for the class. This approach may also support facilities to set up indices on the container sets to improve performance.

The major relational database products now include a number of facilities for optimizing the manner in which queries are processed. Such facilities are less advanced from OODBMSs and care must be taken when specifying queries to ensure the performance is acceptable in an OO scenario.

## Future Trends

Until now, the key benefits of GUIs have been consistency and ease-of-use. Users have learned to rely on icons, menus, and other graphic representations that behave in predictable ways from one program to another within the same software environment. Today's PC operating systems were originally designed to support the needs of a single user working alone at a single computer, however. Most GUIs present the computer as an extension of the user's desk, with folders, documents, a trash can, and other objects such as clocks and in and out baskets that correspond to real objects on real desks. This metaphor has been highly successful with individual users, but it does not meet all the needs of multiple users in various types of work environments working together on a common set of tasks.

Most GUIs for PCs are application centered. To accomplish almost any task, the user must launch a sequence of separate applications to create and process the desired content. Each application comes with its own set of menus and dialog boxes, its own set of tools and data types. Because each type of data is tightly bound to the application that created it, users often have difficulty integrating data from different applications into a single document. Because developers are limited to the application model provided by system software, they basically have only one way to deliver value to their customers.

As segments of the software market mature, application developers become involved in escalating feature wars. Applications become larger and more complex, and each application's tools, menu commands, and other interface elements tend to become more specialized and difficult to learn. Rather than focusing on their work, users must learn many data formats and techniques to run applications and make them work together.

System software extensions such as OLE can alleviate some of the drawbacks of an application-centered interface by allowing developers to divide applications into smaller components (called "servers" in OLE) that have their own separate areas in a single document. To work on such documents, the user activates a component such as a chart in a word-processing document, and the available menus and tools change as appropriate for that component. As application developers use these technologies to divide their applications into smaller pieces, users can interchange components for text, graphics, and spreadsheets rather than using a separate full-featured application for each type of data.

This approach renders some tasks easier. Yet, until all applications are successfully factored, each component will still tend to have separate menus, tools, and data types. Many of them are used for similar purposes such as choosing fonts or drawing lines. As currently implemented on traditional operating systems, the document-centered approach still tends to reflect the underlying application structure.

Perhaps the most important interface trend in object environments involves extending the document-centered approach. Rather than dividing the world into applications and documents, new techniques will emphasize the task to be performed.

Because human labor most frequently consists of a collaborative effort, the human interface or GUI must reflect that reality. A user contends with not only folders and individual documents, but a variety of tools and instruments. Among the tools and instruments are audiovisual representations, markers, notes, and fax machines.

The "power interface" for the coming decade will more closely resemble the Lotus Notes and Internet scenario than anything else. The sense of collaboration, information sharing, and GUI representational flow found in these environments may be the model for a new era in human interface mechanisms.

Chapter 7

# Object-Oriented Applications and Tools

## Benefits of Object-Oriented Applications

The PC era that began in the early 1980s provided a tremendous functionality improvement for the end-user. Applications such as spreadsheets, word processors, and desktop publishing delivered a level of capability never before seen by the end-user community.

No longer did software represent simply a pre-defined set of functions developed to solve a specific problem. Now there were tools – and even tool sets – which could be utilized to address a variable group of functional challenges. As the PC market matured, supplementary products were appended to the original toolsets. This addition resulted in the creation of application frameworks which delivered yet greater power to the end-user.

In the current era, there has been an explosion in raw processing power, an escalating increase in communications capabilities, and most importantly a rise in the use of object technology. Object technology has been introduced into the mainstream more slowly than other elements but offers at least the same degree of benefits over time – if not more in the long run.

With software developers, the benefits of object technology center on reusability through inheritance, modularity, reliability, and all the other benefits. End-users, however, are not directly interested in the reuse of Smalltalk code and the other advantages that appeal to a developer audience.

End-users are more concerned with completing their assigned tasks in an efficient and timely manner. There are three fundamental improvements delivered by object technology that advance the end-user cause. They include:

1. *Improved Flexibility* – OO applications enable users to adapt and customize functionality to meet specific conditions. In fact, objects allow application functionality to be extended beyond its original boundaries, rather than simply reshuffled as with traditional software offerings.

   A cell of a spreadsheet, for example, in conventional methodology will contain a numeric value, text or perhaps a mathematical formula. Such is the extent of its utility. In an object environment, a spreadsheet can represent an array of objects that are instances of classes defined by the user. Each class of cells can be tailored to perform functions ranging from the storage of multimedia-type information to replicating their values in entirely different applications.

2. *Enhanced Integration* – Although the object concept of encapsulation may not interest the end-user to a great degree, it provides that user with improved information sharing across multiple applications. Rather than moving and reformatting data for use among various standalone tools, applications can share objects that contain both data and their accompanying methods.

   OO programs provide end-users with dynamic, not static, integration of information. There is no need to constantly reformat as data is transferred from one tool to another. Data sharing and migration is enhanced by object technology.

3. *Improved Ease-of-use* – In the final analysis, this improved ease-of-use may be the most important benefit of OO applications. The major impetus for this ease-of-use is the greater similarity between real-world problems and object solutions.

Objects more closely model activities in the real world than do conventional procedural methods, which forces a problem to conform to the limitations of a procedural approach. Objects allow applications which contain the main elements of a problem solution to be constructed. In a sense, solutions are pre-defined; there can be objects in a library for the various functional tasks needed to build that solution, with no additional programming necessary by the developer.

As object technology matures, the positive nature of these benefits will only intensify. In a recent Busienss Research Group survey of technology users from more than 60 companies – specifically those considering C/S system implementation – a great majority view objects as the wave of the future as shown in Figures 7.1 and 7.2.

## Figure 7.1 The Object-Oriented Programming Role

OOP will play an increasingly important
role in internally developed C/S applications

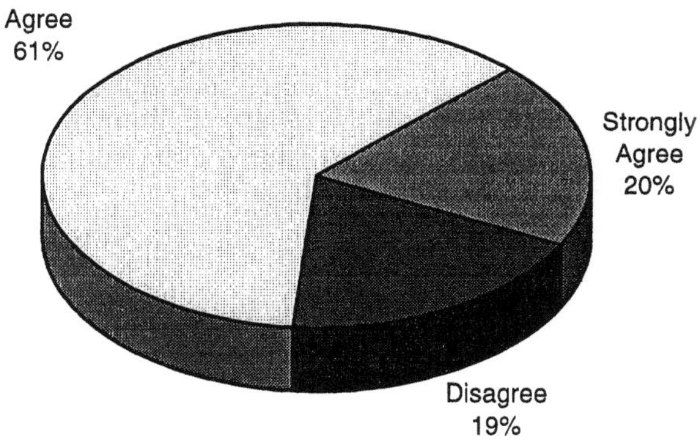


*Source: Business Research Group*

## Figure 7.2 Plans for Object-Oriented Applications

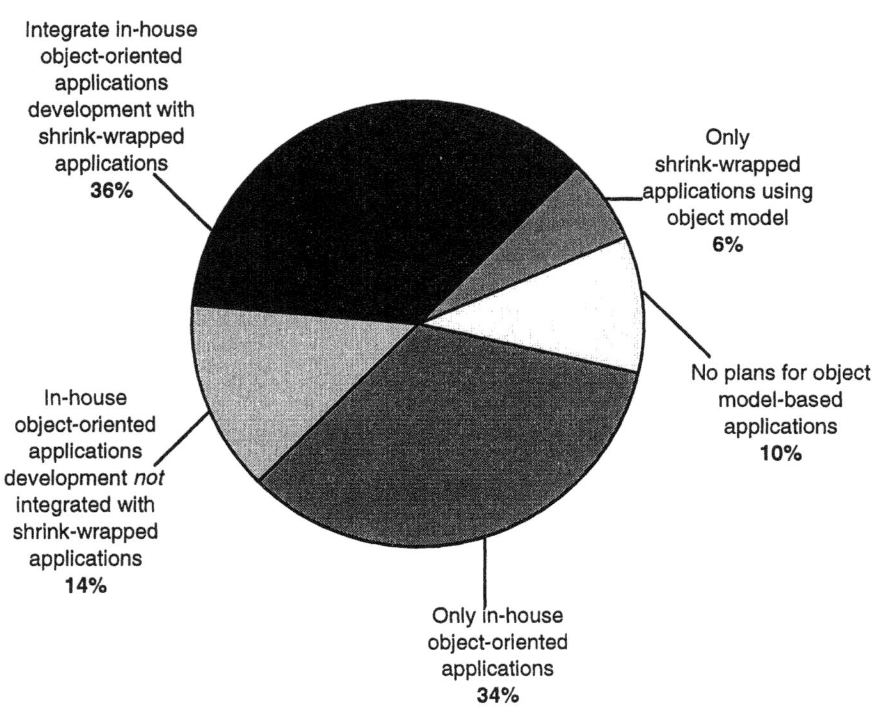


*Source: Business Research Group*

## Application Functionality

It is not surprising that companies such as Microsoft – alone or in collaboration with one or more of its peers – continues searching for better methods to build and manage user applications. This quest, of course, will be a never-ending task because application complexity continues to outpace the ability of software tools to contend with that complexity.

As soon as one or more vendors seem to be gaining ground on any aspect of the software management issue, the nature of that problem metamorphasizes, much like a microbe in biology. One small slice of an attempt at application software management is encompassed in a joint venture between Microsoft and Texas Instruments. They are taking an OLE/repository approach.

　　　　

In today's heterogeneous distributed development environment, information is distributed across the private information stores of tools that generate or use that information. There is often no mechanism for managing a business application as a structured collection of interdependent components, including documentation, code, and data. Even if an application development team uses a shared source code library, the application structure must be inferred from the directory or project structure and file types. It is difficult for a developer to identify opportunities for reuse of designs, code or services or for an administrator to evaluate the impact of a change in one component on other dependent components. Subsets of the information – for example, inventories of third-party components – may be maintained by administrators in specially designed databases so they manage separately from the tools that generate them.

Integral to Microsoft's development tools strategy is the idea of a shared application structure database: A database of descriptive information about the structure of applications integrated with the tools that generate and use the information. This idea is being realized through incremental enhancements to Microsoft's suite of development tools and technologies. Building on their SourceSafe version control system technology, Microsoft plans to combine DBMS technology and new OLE services to deliver improved support in five repository technology areas:

1. *Team development* – Facilities to help designers and programmers manage concurrent activity on different versions and configurations of application design and development.

2. *Reuse* – Facilities for cataloging and locating relevant designs, code, and services (interfaces).

3. *Dependency tracking* – Facilities for establishing and querying relationships between objects.

4. *Tool interoperability* – Facilities that allow analysts, designers, developers, and administrators to move easily between tools across the development life cycle and to manage related versions and configurations of application building blocks.

5. *Data resource management* – Global metadata for an enterprise data warehouse, and a resource (tracking and reuse) library of available services and components.

Today, team development is primarily supported through tool-specific and third-party source code control systems. Reuse and dependency tracking, when available, are facilities specific to the objects understood by a specific tool or tool set. The next step is to formalize and extend these facilities, moving incrementally toward the concept of an extensible, shared repository for heterogeneous tool interoperability. Data resource management will become a natural extension of a dynamic information base managed as an integral part of the design, development, and deployment process.

Microsoft application development tools have private, tool-specific repositories: Development tools such as the Visual Basic programming system and the Visual C++ development system maintain project files of related source code objects; deployment tools such as Systems Management Server maintain information about the packages it is to deploy. Microsoft is working to improve the quality of its development environment by integrating these tool-specific repository functions. Corporations large and small have said development in the enterprise is and always will be heterogeneous. For example, Texas Instrument's Composer by Information Engineering Facility (IEF) may be used to generate application servers whose interfaces are invoked by Visual Basic application code. To deliver on an integrated tool information base, an enterprise repository technology strategy must enable:

- *One API* – A standard set of semantics for repository services and an open interface for invoking them

- *One place* – Data management and integration technology that supports querying repository information and browsing the repository by traversing relationships

- *One representation* – A common tool-information model that allows tools to share information described in the model, and to extend the model to define new types of things

A joint Microsoft-Texas Instruments repository design strategy addresses these requirements. By teaming together on repository strategy, the two companies gain complementary expertise. The industry hopes any resulting product will be more open and extensible.

How successful an industry can be in agreeing on a common information model will depend on sharing a vision of applications and application building blocks. These building blocks include:

- Models of the problem domain such as data models and process models

- Components of the solution domain such as forms, tables, and procedures

- Descriptions of the operational environment such as deployed components, users, platforms, and data

- Relationships among all of them

As an integral part of the repository design activity, Microsoft and Texas Instruments are building a model of business application development based on components that can be distributed across a heterogeneous computing platform as necessary to meet the needs of the enterprise. The next evolution of distributed computing will be characterized by:

- Increased emphasis on team development, in which applications will be constructed from components built by different teams or even different companies

- Heterogeneous tool environment – examples include autonomous teams or companies with their own tool suites, heterogeneous computing platforms, evolving development methodologies, and legacy systems and tools

- Increasingly complex version and configuration management because each component has its own development life cycle

- Increasingly complex management and deployment issues because applications are not just distributed, but rely on shared components, thus blurring the notion of an application as a discrete set of code and data

- Renewed interest in the benefits of reuse, from both technology and business perspectives; for example, consistent usage of business rules across the applications that invoke or enforce them. An enterprise will look for reuse opportunities at all levels: Design, code, component object building blocks, and run-time sharing

Given the complexities in managing applications as shared structures of autonomous components, repository technology will be equally relevant to small corporations and large ones.

The Microsoft-Texas Instruments repository design approach is built on top of a database system. There are several benefits taking this approach, including the ability to:

- Manage non-file objects such as entities, tables, definitions, forms, and files

- Define and manage complex relationships between objects with enforced referential integrity

- Support complex queries, including navigating relationships

- Take advantage of standard database management system facilities such as transactions and back-up and recovery

The design includes three components:

1. *The repository engine* – The run-time support for the repository functions that facilitate metadata manager, including:

   - *Version and configuration management* – Design data evolves, and the repository must store snapshots of that design at different times: The deployed version, the newly released version, and the next release under development. Configurations allow the user to group related versions into sets that have a common purpose such as all the versions in the deployed product. Together, version and configuration management support team development by helping designers and programmers manage concurrent activity.

- *Relationship management* – By establishing different types of relationships between objects, developers can locate related sets of objects, and administrators can track dependencies in the deployed components. Tools can use relationships to navigate between objects.

- *Schema management* – By providing facilities to create and modify object types and classes, tool vendors can extend the repository.

- *Query* – By supporting complex queries over relationships and properties, users can browse the repository, both within the context of a specific configuration and across configurations.

2. *The common information model* – Texas Instruments and Microsoft will define a set of object types and relationships as the basis for tool interoperability. Through the repository engine services, the object types and classes defined in the information model will be extensible.

3. *A set of generic repository tools* – Used for schema management and browsing the repository.

Most of the active use of the repository will occur through the tools used in application design, development, and deployment. Tool interoperability will be supported through a combination of standard database functions such as schemes, queries, and transactions and the information model. The design will support a range of integration options for tools.

The object model for the repository will be based on OLE technology. The repository will be accessed through OLE objects. These objects will support some existing OLE interfaces such as OLE Automation and some new repository-specific interfaces such as those supporting relationships and versions and configuration management.

As a migration strategy, it will be possible to store legacy files and today's OLE objects in the repository. For file objects, the repository will provide basic facilities for check-in/checkout and dependency tracking. However, the more repository-oriented OLE functionality an object supports, the more value the repository can offer in support of browsing and reuse.

As with any application development and implementation activity, there must be an adequate array of aids and tools that help with the overall process. Object technology, however, is still in a nascent stage, not bereft of tools, but not overflowing with such necessities either.

Tools vendors and their related products are expanding at a rapid pace, however, although some support areas are still relatively weak. Among these areas are system integration, database support, and even class library aids. A sampling of OO tool vendors and their products is shown in Table 7.1.

### Table 7.1 Object-Oriented Tool Vendors and Their Products

| Vendor | Product | Web Site* |
|---|---|---|
| CenterLine Software | ObjectCenter | centerline.com |
| Versant Object Technology | Versant Argos | versant.com |
| Next Software | NextStep, OpenStep | next.com |
| Hewlett-Packard | SoftBench | hp.com |
| Neuron Data | Elements Environment | neurondata.com |
| Rational Software | Rational Rose | rational.com |
| IBM | Visual Age | ibm.com |
| MicroFocus | Visual Object COBOL | microfocus.com |
| ParcPlace Digitalk | VisualWorks | parcplace.com |

*Note: All Web site address locations are preceded by http://www.

## Case Study

What follows is one example of an implementation of object technology in a large company (whose name has been changed) serving thousands of customers. There are principles manifested here which could apply to almost any setting, large or small.

South Western Gas (SWGAS) is one of the largest oil and gas distributors in the United States. Similar to many large companies, the Denver-based SWGAS installed mainframe-based accounting, billing, and customer service systems in the late 1960s and 1970s. In 1988, these mainframe-based systems received a new PC front-end.

In a project that began in December 1991 and is still underway, SWGAS is making the transition from that system (PC front-end/mainframe back-end) to a new OOT-based system. This new system has a PC front-end, greater dispersion, and integration of back-end services. It was created to provide SWGAS with a flexible customer-focused system that adapts well to change. The current deregulation in the gas industry is requiring a greater customer focus and creating the opportunity for many new service offerings. The original system was designed for one service offering: Bundled gas sales. The new system will enable SWGAS to offer customers choices in service and service levels.

Specifically, the system allows the SWGAS administrators to take orders for new service, follow-up on billing issues, and provide the field force with information on starting and stopping service to its customers. When completed, it will serve 1,200 primary and 900 secondary SWGAS employees.

The SWGAS development team was faced with several significant challenges. One challenge was maintaining favorable aspects of the former system while adding new functionality. The 1988 PC facelift solved many problems and was deemed a successful upgrade to the existing mainframe system.

The initial challenge presented to the SWGAS team was upgrading the character-based PC front-end's functionality without losing current functions, incurring high retraining costs for users. It was crucial to develop a detailed design and architectural framework before programmers began writing code.

The design particularly benefited from the continued involvement of actual users, who reviewed the code produced by the development team. SWGAS administrators used a command line system that allowed user access.

After the team analyzed the problems and potential approaches that would address their situation, they settled upon an OOT strategy. Such a strategy allowed them to more easily develop and implement the project in pieces, while testing and modifying each along the way. It also gave them the flexibility to incrementally upgrade each part of the system, while leaving the other parts intact.

The team saw how they could achieve a high degree of reuse even in the early stages of the build phase of the project with the proper initial design. However, one large obstacle had to be overcome. One of the big problems was in producing metrics that made sense. From the OOT-based analysis and design right through project implementation, the OOT approach did not readily lend itself to the familiar project management tools to which SWGAS management was accustomed. Before the project team could gain the backing of upper management, it had to develop its own metrics.

The development team was challenged by management to demonstrate it could effectively deliver this project both on budget and with a low degree of technical risk. To accomplish this, the team rethought the development process, attempted to retain the user-friendly aspects of the old system, and sought to include maximum user input on the new system. This led to joint workgroups composed of developers and users who mutually worked on all aspects of the new interface.

These workgroups defined the new user interface, then linked that interface to an object model and an underlying repository. Central to this effort was the ability of the users and developers to draw a strict relationship between screen objects the users could feel comfortable with and the underlying object model. A user-familiar object would be displayed on a PC screen. Through the manipulation of that object, the user would invoke actions in the underlying object repository that would then be transparent to the user and invoke processes on the mainframe.

This development approach encouraged early user involvement and established a strong conceptual basis for OOT. The team defined 400 windows to construct during the project, which represent common business functions for SWGAS. Each window is built up from many objects and therefore represents an opportunity for reuse of objects from window to window, although reuse was not a major goal of the development team.

To produce all the necessary software for these windows, reusing components among the windows became imperative. The team ran several pilot projects testing its ability to forecast and monitor the OOT development process and meet user expectations. The issue of maximizing reuse was difficult to manage, particularly between the many windows and underlying mainframe applications that supplied information used in the screen objects. The collected customer data is augmented with billing or financial information from the mainframe accounting program.

An issue which quickly arose in the design portion of this project was the need to establish the correct level of granularity for objects. The team recognized the need for several levels of granularity. The lowest level of granularity might not be reusable unless aggregated to a higher level. This level would be exemplified by the ability to represent a "customer name" as an object, but only being able to reuse that object as part of an aggregated higher level object called "customer profile." The customer profile object would then be reused in multiple user screens. When changes were made to any of the component objects by other administrators or through the processing of programs on the mainframe, the customer profile object would transparently reflect these changes to the user. The advantage of this design: The administrator always has immediate access to the most recent information in a manner that minimizes required training on the system.

This type of early design discussion made reuse at the proper level of granularity much easier between the many windows and other components of the project. Once the pilot projects were successfully completed, the project was officially launched. The project design, which began in June 1992, was completed in September 1993; the construction phase was completed in 1994; and the systems testing then commenced. The system installation was completed in 1995.

It was clear that adjustments in process had to be made. In addition to providing adequate metrics, the group had to:

- Create a new set of testing procedures for regression testing each completed component, rather than waiting and testing entire programs

- Completely involve users in all phases of the development process. In this case, outside consultant lent the experience necessary to guide the team through the many architectural and methodological choices necessary in the early stages of the project.

Thus far, the results for SWGAS are a project that is on track, on budget, and meeting with an enthusiastic response from end-users. The development team is delivering increased functionality through the creation of windows that display objects familiar to end-users. This new functionality is delivered in a familiar way users can easily learn and use. On the technical side, the team spent far longer in the design and architectural development phase than would be necessary in a traditional procedural development project. This time has been made up in the production phase by the reuse of objects from window to window.

## Future Trends

Perhaps the largest challenge facing technology developers and users in the years ahead is integration of legacy applications into new systems. As can be seen in Figure 7.3, up to 49% of new development projects include legacy code reuse. The vast majority of these projects will employ components of some type.

## Figure 7.3 Percentage of Legacy Reuse

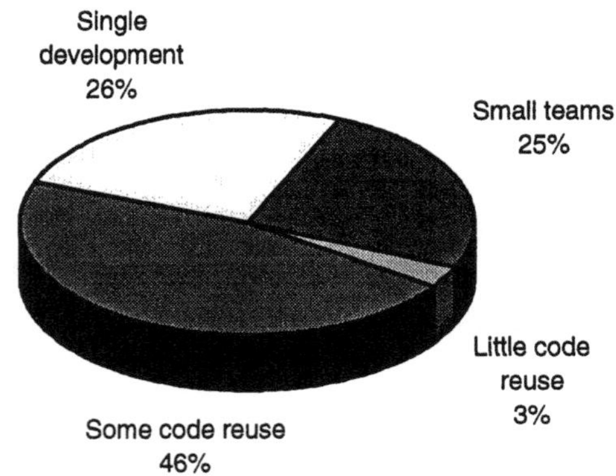


*Source: IDC*

Components are self-contained entities with clearly delineated interfaces. Although the definition resembles the definition of an object, components are not necessarily just objects. In fact, there are few component developers who do not use object technology.

  

Other attributes common to components: They perform very specific functions and can be routinely integrated into like subsystems. Component libraries have evolved from items such as linked lists and low-level math libraries to GUI routines and printer modules. Now, components exist within frameworks such as Next Software's NextStep. From the perspective of object technology, classes combine to form components which then combine to form frameworks (see Figure 7.4).

## Figure 7.4 Object Technology Levels

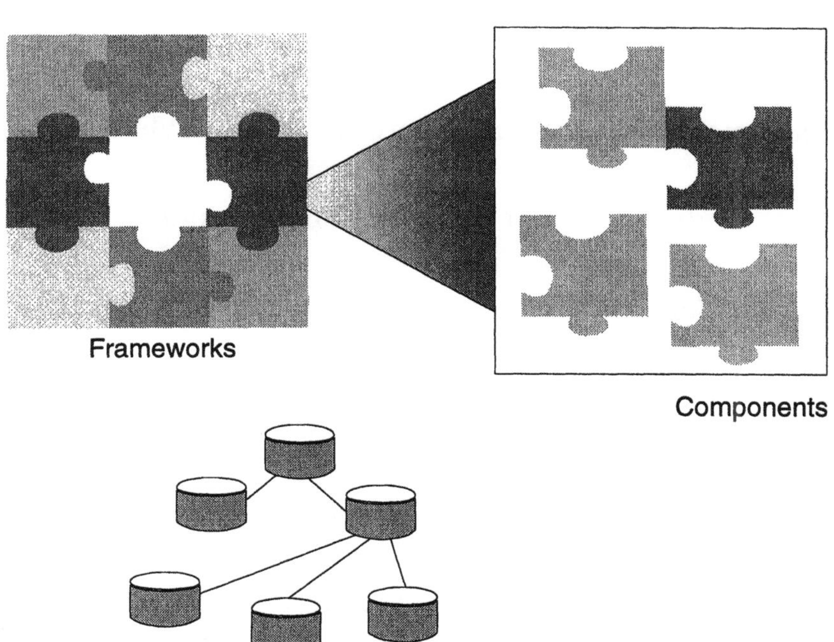


When it comes to legacy application reuse, components and object-technology considerably advance the cause. Through the use of wrappers which allow existing modules to be "containerized" and given a straightforward object-based interface, older systems can be integrated into the processing flow along with new developments. When modifications must be made to the containerized legacy system, they can then be imposed through object technology without disturbing surrounding modules. In effect, the old applications have been "objectified."

A consortium of component advocates has been formed. This group, called the ComponentWare Consortium (CWC), it is focused on delivering validated,

---

reusable software components (called ComponentWare) to system developers. CWC also is offering a technique labeled Information Factory Methodology, which is intended to guide developers toward a distributed set of encapsulated components assembled from various legacy applications.

CWC is supporting CORBA and OLE/COM. Its vendor adherents and practitioners include I-Kinetics of Burlington, Massachusetts; Iona Technology of Marlboro, Massachusetts; NetLinks Technology of Nashua, New Hampshire; and Heuristicrat Research of Berkeley, California.

Some of its initial component offerings include:

- *Data Management* - ObjectStore, Informix, Oracle, Sybase, and Frame

- *Development Modules* - Visual Basic and PowerBuilder

- *Application Modules* - Microsoft Word, Access, and Excel; Lotus 1-2-3, Quattro

Component-based development will continue to grow. Organizations are seeking packaged offerings that can be assembled into working system solutions. The component inventory will expand to include industry-specific modules that will appeal to a targeted audience. Software development with components will be able to manage greater functional complexity (see Table 7.2).

## Table 7.2 Vendor Products and Their Web Site Addresses

| Vendor Product | Web Site Address * |
|---|---|
| CenterLine Software – ObjectCenter | centerline.com |
| Versant Object Technology – Versant Argos | versant.com |
| Next Software – NextStep – OpenStep | next.com |
| HPSoftBench | hp.com |
| Neuron DataElements Environment | neurondata.com |
| Rational Software – Rational Rose | rational.com |
| IBM – Visual Age | ibm.com |
| MicroFocus – Visual Object | cobol.com |
| ParcPlace/Digitalk – VisualWorks | parcplace.com |

*Note: All Web site address locations are preceded by http://www.

# Chapter 8

# Object-Oriented Analysis and Design

## Background and Benefits

The evolution of object technology is not unlike other new methods that have emerged in the world of computing since the days of vacuum tubes and machine language coding. This evolution is particularly true in the arena of OO analysis and design (OOAD) methods.

OO notations and/or processes for OO development have been introduced at a rapid pace in the last few years. Upwards of two dozen OO methods claim to support a complete development lifecycle. Thus, the traditional Tower of Babel is manifested in the qualities of inconsistency, disharmony, and non-cooperation among the variety of techniques available.

This disjointed array of notations is confusing to novice implementors of object technology. "Method wars," similar in nature to endless other wars in the computing arena, are now appearing. The C++ versus Smalltalk battles waged among language users is an example.

Methods abound in the field of OOAD. There are Shlaer/Mellor, Rumbaugh, Booch and Coad/Yourdon methods. Some of these methods grew out a perceived need, some emerged to manage a unique set of requirements, and one or two of the two dozen known techniques were initiated to serve political ends.

A single core notation is needed in the OOAD environment in this post-adolescent phase of object technology; one notation that can be expanded

---

upon by individual practitioners, but which maintains a standard set of central principles. This need is identical to the need for some degree of standardization experienced by every other emerging technology innovation during the recent decades.

What are some of the seminal attributes needed by OOAD mechanisms? These capabilities which serve as a starting point include:

- The identification of objects and definitions of classes

- The organization of classes in a hierarchical manner

- The issue of class reuse

- The role of components and application frameworks within the object design plan

An OOAD methodology begins with a set of class definitions. Each class has an aggregation of methods it defines and a list of objects to which its instances pass messages. This exercise is complete – at least in a conceptual sense – when each class, method, and message is explicitly defined.

In real-world situations, designers rarely start from scratch. There will be existing class libraries that will be leveraged for future development. This after all, is the essence of object technology; pre-defined resources can be exploited in an advantageous manner.

OOAD techniques tend to result in systems adaptable to change. The one constant in all of these situations is change. It is endemic, and objects are perhaps best suited to handle change. When change occurs, the unique property of inheritance promotes reuse and extension of the existing design approach.

Object technology's other attributes of polymorphism and encapsulation are also a positive force in system analysis, design, and development. Because methods and accompanying data are containerized within objects, multiple planning and implementation teams can simultaneously function on the same project without the heavy burden of perpetual interaction.

OOAD consists of many methods and notations. In the final analysis, however, it must produce a set of outputs that advance the overall object technology implementation effort. Among these outputs are a set of class specifications with the delineation of an overall system structure that incorporates the classes.

The class specifications for each class must include:

- The attributes of the class

- The method interface to the class; for example, the services an object of the class can be called upon to provide and the parameters supplied and returned in an invocation of that service. The interface definition should also note rules or preconditions that affect the operation of the method so the method can only complete successfully if certain attributes have particular values

- Descriptions of the processing required to provide each service for which objects of the class may be responsible

- The position of the class within the class hierarchy. This determines which attributes and methods are defined or overridden specifically for the class and which are inherited from other classes

The overall delineation of the software system must address a wide range of issues covering both logical and physical aspects of the system implementation. The main logical requirement is a definition of the flow of control through the system for each external input to the system, for example, the object methods that are called and the order in which they are called. This is the most complex area of the design due to the various combinations of external events, object methods, and object states that must be considered. It will often also involve the identification of further objects for which new class specifications must be produced.

In physical terms, the overall system specification must address such issues as:

- Distributing the system across machines and/or processes

- The methods of communication between processes

- The data management strategy

- The use and integration of external class libraries

To achieve these outputs, a number of activities must be performed:

1. *An overview statement of requirements must be produced through discussions with users* – This will normally be a natural language statement, although it may contain outline diagrams of key concepts (which will probably become objects or classes) and the interaction between them.

2. *The objects and classes must be identified* – This is usually undertaken through a study of the overview statement of requirements and through further discussions with users and among the analysis team. The objects and classes will normally be represented in a graphical form, as this allows relationships between objects to be clearly expressed.

3. *The services to be provided by each class must be determined* – This may be done by working through examples of the processing that the system is required to perform. This activity also records the collaborations between objects and eventually provides the framework for the overall system design.

4. *The attributes and associations of the classes must be defined* – This tends to be an ongoing activity as the various functional requirements are revisited. The associations will normally be shown in graphical format and the attributes will often be shown on the object diagrams.

5. *The response of objects of each class to events must be determined* – These events will be incoming calls to their methods, and the state of the objects when the message is received, and their state after method invocation.

6. *The processing involved in each method must be defined* – This may be portrayed through some form of diagram.

7. *An inheritance hierarchy of the classes must be determined* – This is undertaken through a review of the work performed in defining the classes.

8. *The environment in which the system is to be run must be defined and additional objects needed to support the environment must be determined* – These objects will provide services in communications, user interfaces, and data storage. The new objects must be fully defined.

9. *A division into subsystems and processes must be derived* – Considering the level of communications, such as service requests, between the various objects that have been defined. This also determines the structure of the controlling software that instigates services from objects in response to an external event.

10. *The formal design specification for each class must be completed* – This consists of compiling the work done on each class during other activities.

11. *An overall design specification covering areas such as distribution of processing, data storage, system interfaces, and communications must be produced.*

## Defining Objects and Classes

In the comparatively brief duration that object technology has been in the mainstream, numerous techniques have been created for the fundamental step of defining objects and classes. One of the earliest was developed by Grady Booch of the Booch OOAD notation. While more complex methods have since emerged, it is worth examining this earlier model because it so clearly demonstrates the principles of object design.

The design of any OO system begins with objects. Defining these objects is the prime task of OOAD. Booch suggested this approach back in the early 1980s:

- Start with a prose description of the system to be built. The nouns in this prose are potential classes of objects. Verbs within the same prose identify methods (or processes) that will reside in the objects. This list of classes and methods (for example, nouns and verbs) form the nucleus to start the design task.

- The preceding approach is a "rule of thumb," generic approach to object and class creation. It is understood that not all nouns, for example, will necessarily become objects. English prose is not a good mechanism to achieve perfect precision. There will be some nouns and some verbs that will be external to the OOAD experience. It is expected that a design team will possess enough insight to differentiate between key words and non-key words.

- After objects are identified, there should be a list of attributes associated with each object. For example, if the object represents a document, then attributes such as create, delete, and save can be associated with it. These same attributes are the verbs in the prose description. They become potential methods in the object model.

- The final part of this basic approach is to define the interfaces among objects. Standards such as CORBA become important when implementing such interfaces.

In a general sense, this "write a paragraph" (or more) approach is basic, fundamental, and sound, but it does not cover all contingencies when defining classes and objects. For example, some verbs may need to be defined as classes, dependent on the nature of the function to be performed.

Some further rules of thumb for identifying classes have been promulgated by experienced practitioners in this field. Among them:

- Identify classes that occur naturally in the problem domain

- Design methods that have a single function

- If faced with extending an existing method – do not build a new one

- Avoid lengthy methods; keep it simple

- Try to design for the greater good, such as for the class library, rather than just for a current application

Pre-defined class libraries can obviate much of the preceding steps. The challenge is to find such a resource, know which parts are valuable, and exploit it sufficiently so the time spent seeking and deciphering it are worthwhile.

## Object Use

There probably has been more object usage work performed with Microsoft's OLE than with any other vehicle available. For one, it has been around a long time, at least from an object technology sense. Secondly, it has been promoted fairly successfully by Microsoft, giving it a certain degree of momentum.

Thus, when reviewing a form of object use, OLE might be the place to start. Not because it is superior to competing methodologies, but due to its ubiquitous presence. OLE's approach to support for enterprise development is indicative of its ambitious goals for the future. This support is based on encapsulation, 32-bit addressing, multitier architecture, and enforcement of business rules.

Building on the concept of the Visual Basic Control, OLE technology helps facilitate large-scale code reuse by providing the opportunity for encapsulation. Through encapsulation, a component developer can place specific, tested software functionality in an environment protected from penetration by other software while providing a well-defined public interface for methods and properties that can be exposed to other developers. Through the OLE technique for defining specifications for intercomponent communication, independently developed components can interoperate seamlessly even if neither of them has "knowledge" of the other. The components are independent of the tools that use them. By packaging functionality as OLE components, enterprise developers can make such functionality reusable throughout the organization by any tool supporting interoperability with OLE automation servers. Such tools include all the Microsoft development tools, Office for Windows 95, and numerous third-party tools.

OLE components are maintained separately and independently from OLE client applications and can be accessed from anywhere in the enterprise. OLE components are packaged as separate dynamic link libraries (DLLs) or executables. They are not compiled into the application that uses them; only the call to the OLE component is included. Installing an updated DLL or execution (EXE) file on a processor and then updating the registry ensures its enhanced functionality will be available to calling applications. There is no need to recompile the calling application.

This feature enables multiple levels of control. For example, a department can control its own application while retrieving the most recent business rules from an updated OLE component automatically installed by the Systems Management Server (SMS) component of the Microsoft Back Office integrated family of server software.

OLE components written to support 32-bit processors and the Microsoft Windows 95 or Windows NT OS also can help improve the performance and security of enterprise applications. Such components can take full advantage of the 32-bit addressing, the more powerful instruction set, the increased security, and the multitasking and multithreading that current processors and operating systems provide. In turn, such components can substantially increase the performance of the applications in which they are used. This is particularly important because shared OLE components can be called by multiple applications and therefore must operate at peak performance.

Traditionally, multiple applications might share a single database, with each application contacting the database individually. Following this approach, each application needs some understanding of the database's underlying structure, its data elements, and its stored procedures. Unfortunately, changes to the database can directly affect many different applications. Without using a central registry database to track those applications in a position to be affected by database changes, such changes can create an administrative nightmare for database administrators and developers alike.

An OLE-based three-tier architecture is not affected in the same manner. By providing an OLE component that interacts with the database used by multiple applications, individual developers must know only about those data elements exposed as properties, which they can read or update (with the appropriate permission) by calling standard methods for creating, changing or deleting records.

In today's enterprises, data can originate from many sources: Mainframes, RDBMSs, spreadsheets, word processing documents, the Internet, and flat files. An OLE-based approach can encapsulate all these data types, protecting data users from any need to understand or interact with the various data sources.

Visual Basic Enterprise Edition includes a technology known as Remote Automation, which enables developers to deploy OLE objects across the network without any changes to the coding of the OLE automation server (no changes are required to the client, either). This technique facilitates scalability and makes the encapsulated data uniformly accessible across the network. Also, within OLE technology is support for an approach whereby database changes affect only one piece of code. As a result, internal database structures are of no consequence to the application developer. Structural changes to the database such as migration of a table from one database to another affect only one piece of code: The OLE component. Such changes are transparent to all the object's users, whose code is not touched.

In addition, OLE-based business rules can be called identically from any application supporting OLE automation servers without regard to programming language and without knowledge of the server's internals. This is useful in that different tools may be needed for different applications and no one tool can meet all needs. However, all tools that support calling OLE automation servers call them identically. This approach eliminates the need for writing a multitude of proprietary wrappers for accessing the same data from multiple solutions created with different tools. In turn, development is speeded and simplified, and identical access is provided to the power user, the corporate developer, and the component builder. This is especially important in an enterprise environment, where different tools may be used in different parts of the organization.

On another front, Microsoft is preparing an OO framework to support network and system management. OLE-based objects are being created to assist vendors in linking all important hardware devices and applications.

The framework is based on the NT Server update, dubbed Cairo, and delivery is scheduled for late 1997.

Under a plan labeled OLE Management Services (MS), Microsoft is building an NT Server-based management repository, along with a set of generic OLE MS objects. These objects can be tailored to an individual vendor's requirements.

The OLE MS objects would communicate events to the management repository. OLE-enabled applications can access the data in the repository. Conversion utilities for managing simple network management protocol (SNMP), desktop management interface (DMI), and common management information protocol/common management information services (CMIP/CMIS) are being produced. That converted data will be available to any OLE-enabled management application. Figure 8.1 illustrates the interrelationships represented in this plan.

## Figure 8.1 OLE Management Services

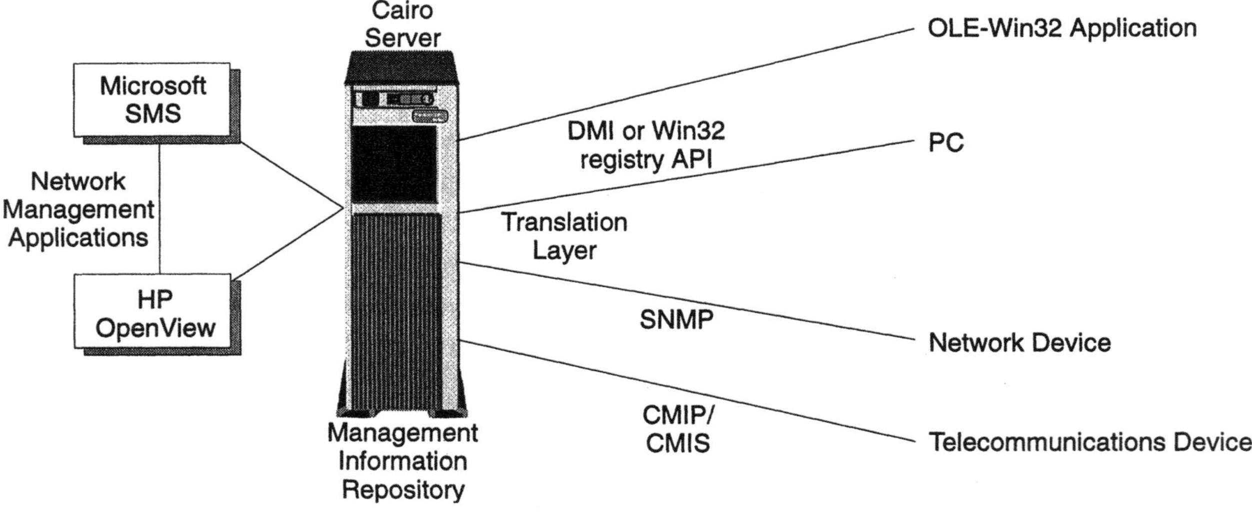


## Analysis and Design Methods

This is the area where short-sighted managers and developers often like to get through quickly. They want to begin work on the programming and implementation phase as quickly as possible to produce a working system. OOAD is, however, the foundation for future application success.

Shortcutting one's labors here lays the groundwork for failure in project development.

As procedural programming relies on some form of structured analysis and design methodology, so too does object technology have its analysis and design techniques. There are, in fact, numerous methods available in the marketplace. Some perform analysis, some assist with design, many manage both activities, and may even get into the programming area itself.

Methodologies, of course, are conceptual guidelines within the framework of object technology. There are tools that implement such methods. Table 8.1 shows a representation of these tools, along with the methods used by each tool. The list is representative only. There are more methods than shown and new tools constantly enter the marketplace.

### Table 8.1 Object-Oriented Application Development Tools and Methods

| Product/Vendor | Supports (Methods) | | | | | |
|---|---|---|---|---|---|---|
| Tools | Booch | Coad/ Yourdon | OOIE (Martin/Odell) | OMT (Rumbaugh) | Shlaer/ Mellor | RDD (Wirts-Brock) |
| Atriom / Semaphore | ● | | ● | ● | | |
| BOCS / Berard Software | | | | | | |
| EasyCASE Plus / Evergreen | | | | | ● | |
| EiffelCase / ISE | | | | | | |
| Excelerator II / Intersolve | | | ● | ● | | ● |
| HOMSuite / Hatteras Software | | | | | | ● |
| Iconix Object Modeler Power Tools/ Iconix | ● | ● | | ● | | |
| ILOG KADS Tool / ILOG | | | | ● | | |
| Intelligent Software Factory / Reich Technologies | | | | | | |
| IPSYS Toolbuilder / IPSYS | | | | | ● | |
| Macanalyst Expert / Excel Software | ● | ● | | ● | ● | |
| Object-Designer / Chen & Associates | | | | | | |

| Product/Vendor | Supports (Methods) | | | | | |
|---|---|---|---|---|---|---|
| Tools | Booch | Coad/Yourdon | OOIE (Martin/Odell) | OMT (Rumbaugh) | Shlaer/Mellor | RDD (Wirts-Brock) |
| Object Engineering Workbench/ Innovative Software GmbH | | | ● | | | |
| ObjectMaker/Mark V Systems | ● | ● | ● | ● | ● | ● |
| ObjectModeler/Iconix | ● | ● | | ● | | |
| Object Team/Cadre Technologies | | | | ● | ● | |
| Objecteering/Softeam | | | | | | |
| Objec time/Objec Time | | | | | | |
| Object System/Designer/Palladlo | ● | | | | | |
| Objectory/Objectory | | | | | | |
| OMTool /Advanced Concepts Center | | | | ● | | |
| OMW/IntelliCorp | | | ● | | | |
| OOA/OOD Tools/Object International | | ● | | | | |
| Paradigm Plus/ProtoSoft | ● | ● | | ● | ● | |
| Ptech/Ptech | | | ● | | | |
| Rose/Rational Software | ● | | | | | |
| S-CASE/MultiQuest | ● | | | | | |
| Select OMT/Select Software Tools | | | ● | | | |
| SES/objectbench/SES | | | | | ● | |
| Software through Pictures/IDE | ● | | | ● | | |
| System Architect/Popkin | ● | ● | | ● | ● | |
| Teamwork/Cadre Technologies | | | | | ● | |
| TurboCASE/Structsoft | | | | | ● | ● |
| VSF/Virtual Software Factory | ● | ● | ● | | | ● |

The first step in the analysis phase is to identify and define objects. Procedures are then molded around objects which results in a design based on a uniform hierarchy of object classes. Fundamentally, the emphasis here is to describe only those objects that have relevance in the real-world model being addressed by the resulting application.

Once a set of object classes has been identified, then invalid, inappropriate or irrelevant classes should be culled from the aggregation. Much of this work centers on removing redundant classes. The final analysis phase product will be a set of valid objects for use in the problem domain.

In the design phase of an OOAD exercise, attention is focused on identifying appropriate objects for data management, task management, and GUI domains. The latter domain, for example, will be represented by a multitude of classes. These include display boxes, buttons, containers and numerous types of window images.

Three methods are used in the tool world more than others. The Booch Method, the Rumbaugh Method (the OMT), and Shlaer/Mellor (also called OO System Analysis). All of these methods are merging to a degree, particularly those from Booch and Rumbaugh who are both employed by Rational Software Corp.

Whichever method is employed, it is vital that the OOAD function be given sufficient time and resources to build a solid foundation for future development. This solid foundation will pay dividends in the programming and implementation phase.

# Chapter 9

# Standards

## All about CORBA

CORBA is OMG's architecture (see Figure 9.1) for routing objects. At the very core of CORBA is the ORB supports multiple languages and platforms. CORBA 2.x uses TCP/IP as its communications protocol for distributed objects, with DCE as an optional alternative.

**Figure 9.1 CORBA Architecture**

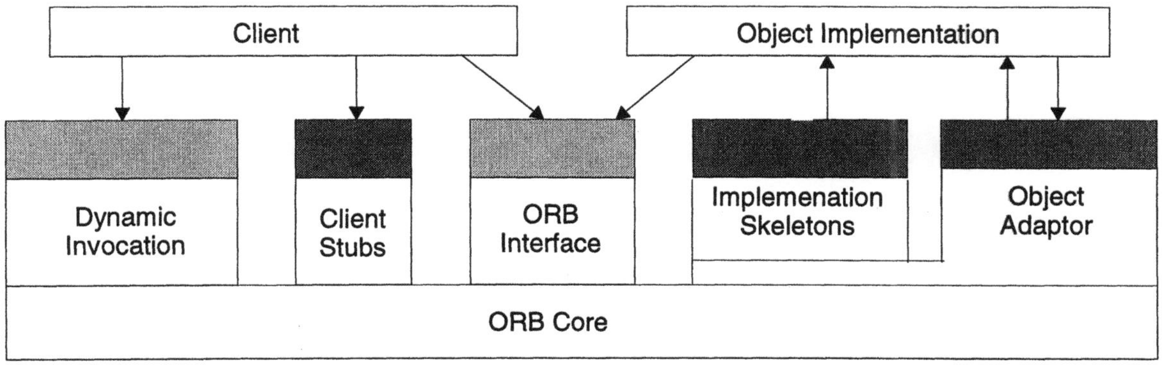

The OMG was founded in 1989 by a handful of vendors. Among them were IBM, Digital, HP, SunSoft, and Iona Technologies. The group has now expanded to more than 500 members.

In late 1990, OMG published its first specification entitled the Object Management Architecture Guide. This was updated in 1992. A major revision followed in 1995, which stressed ORB interoperability, considered a vital element by object technology implementors.

There are four key elements in the CORBA model. They are:

1. *Object Request Broker* – An ORB is basically an interconnection bus among objects. The ORB interacts and submits requests to differing objects. In this way, clients are shielded from the processes needed to communicate with other objects. An interface definition language (IDL), along with related APIs, enable C/S-type object interactions within a single manifestation of an ORB. CORBA 2.0 introduced interoperability among ORBs from different vendors.

2. *Object Services* – There are numerous object services as shown in Figure 9.2. They are each bundled with IDL-compliant interfaces. The OMG has been adding additional services over the years. For example, services such as security, query, licensing, time, and properties are recent additions.

3. *Horizontal CORBA facilities*

4. *Vertical CORBA facilities*

# Figure 9.2 CORBA Standards

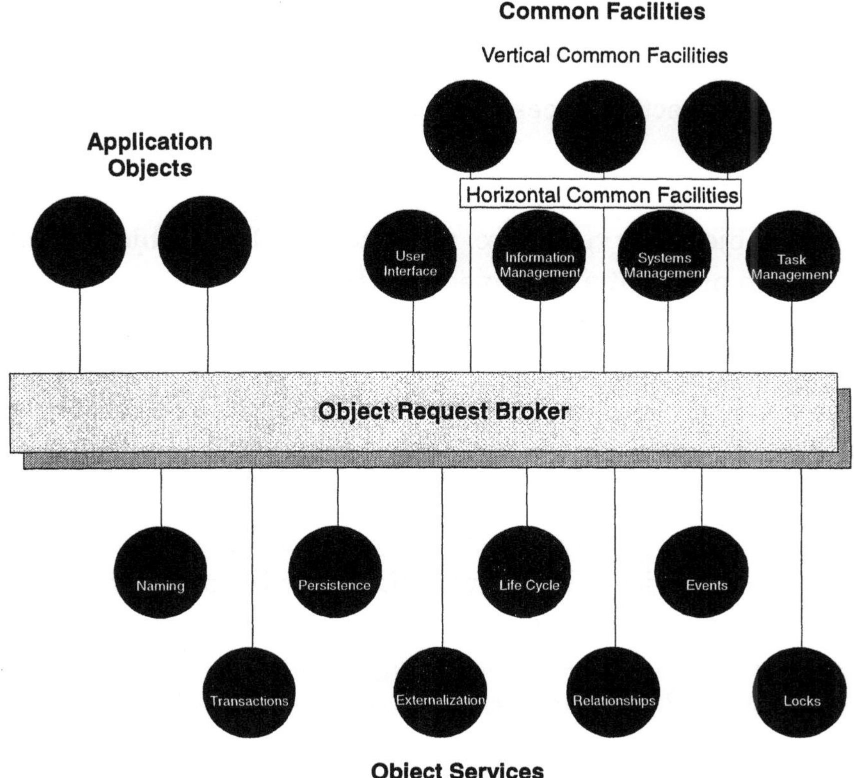


Functions performed by Object Services displayed in Figure 9.2 are:

- The naming object service maps a readable name in the form of a string to an object relative to its context

- Event management object services refer to the asynchronous communication of different CORBA objects with one another

- Persistent object services insure a CORBA object outlives its creator. This way, if the object is called at a later time, the methods will be in place for that object to start up and continue to be used. This feature is used when a host fails abruptly or when rebooting

- Life-cycle object services determine the techniques for an object's creation and termination

- Concurrency object services are used for distributed locks on a given object. The distributed locks enable the object to be used in a global manner

- Externalization object services refer to collecting objects and transporting them as packets

- Relationship object services are used for CORBA object modeling, for example, Booch or Rumbaugh object methods

- Transaction object services allow multiple objects to share a transaction. These transactions are interoperable with X/Open distributed transaction processing (DTP) systems

Higher level object services and interfaces are common facilities. They extend the aforesaid object services. They are IDL-defined components which specify the rules of interaction for application objects. There are vertical facilities whose IDL-defined interfaces support aggregations of interacting objects within vertical markets such as banking, retail, and health.

Horizontal facilities manage four basic activities: User interface services such as OLE and OpenDoc control on-screen manipulations; information management services support compound document storage and data interchange, again much like similar functions in OLE and OpenDoc; systems management services handle interfaces used to control distributed objects; and task management services encompass a series of actions such as work flow, scripting, and general rules.

The IDL-defined objects built to utilize the CORBA architecture are application objects. They are endemic to end-user applications. They leverage the services provided by the ORB, Object Services, and Common Facilities.

The CORBA specification defines an IDL for defining the interfaces of objects in the architecture. IDL provides syntax for specifying the signatures of externally-visible operations that can be performed by an object supporting that interface. The CORBA IDL syntax is generally based on C++, and a host language binding to C is defined in OMG specifications.

The CORBA IDL plays a similar role to that of the IDL in a RPC facility. IDL specifications can be compiled to produce client stubs (for clients to call object operations) and implementation skeletons (essentially server stubs); one stub and skeleton is defined for each operation supported by an object. The use of a compiled client stub to access an object interface is referenced as the static interface. A dynamic invocation interface (DII) is also provided that allows clients to construct requests at run-time to objects whose types might not have been known at compile-time. Both static interfaces and the DII use an object's implementation skeleton on the object (server) side; static and dynamic requests are semantically equivalent methods of invoking operations on objects.

Objects are made known to the ORB by being registered with an object adapter. The object adapter uses the implementation skeletons of the various operations defined by the object implementation to call these operations when handling a request directed at the object. The definition of a basic object adapter (BOA) is contained in CORBA. The BOA is generally designed to handle objects that are independently constructed, and must be handled individually by the adapter. The CORBA specification also identifies other types of adapters that might be more appropriate for objects implemented in different ways. For example, CORBA identifies a DBMS object adapter that would be more appropriate for objects defined within a database environment.

The CORBA specification also defines the concepts of an implementation repository and an interface repository. The implementation repository is a database of information about object implementations that can be used by an object adapter. The interface repository is a database of object interface definitions currently known to the architecture that can be used in defining new applications or accessed at run-time by clients to construct dynamic requests.

Of particular importance to CORBA technology is its IDL. IDL, as cited earlier, allows CORBA to be defined and mapped to particular languages such as C++. The definition consists of the methods and parameters that make up the object interface.

IDL is a separate language within the CORBA standard. It describes the interfaces that client objects use when they need to access an object implementation. The IDL has been mapped to languages such as C, C++, Smalltalk, Ada, and Java.

The key to CORBA's future is the measure of support it finds in the marketplace. The technology has tremendous potential to simplify application development (although the CORBA learning process itself is anything but simple) and promote code reuse. OLE is a powerful competitor, albeit a lesser mechanism for distributed OO implementation.

Many object systems follow the object model represented in CORBA. Among them: IBM's SOM, HP's ORB+, Digital's ObjectBroker, and Iona Technology's Orbix.

### All about OLE

Unlike the cast of hundreds associated with CORBA, OLE is strictly a Microsoft creation. It supports application interoperability and allows users to create compound documents with varying formats. OLE services are built around the COM which emerged from the DCE RPC specification.

At present, object linking and embedding (OLE) supports only Windows applications. This differentiates it starkly from the broad heterogeneity sought by CORBA. Digital has been working on an OLE to UNIX port.

Before proceeding any further, it is helpful to review the multiple meanings of the COM appellation. OLE 2.x COM is one COM. It specifies interfaces between component objects within a single application or between applications, but not across a network.

The second COM is entitled DCOM. It is the distributed version of OLE's COM. This newer, distributed COM provides communication transparency between components across networks. It builds on top of DCE's RPC.

As with CORBA, both COMs require all interfaces be specified using IDL. Microsoft's IDL, however, is not CORBA-compliant.

Figure 9.3 illustrates the interrelationships of the OLE architecture. As can be seen, OLE software services are built on top of COM. These OLE services are often referred to as object-embedded system services.

## Figure 9.3 OLE Architecture

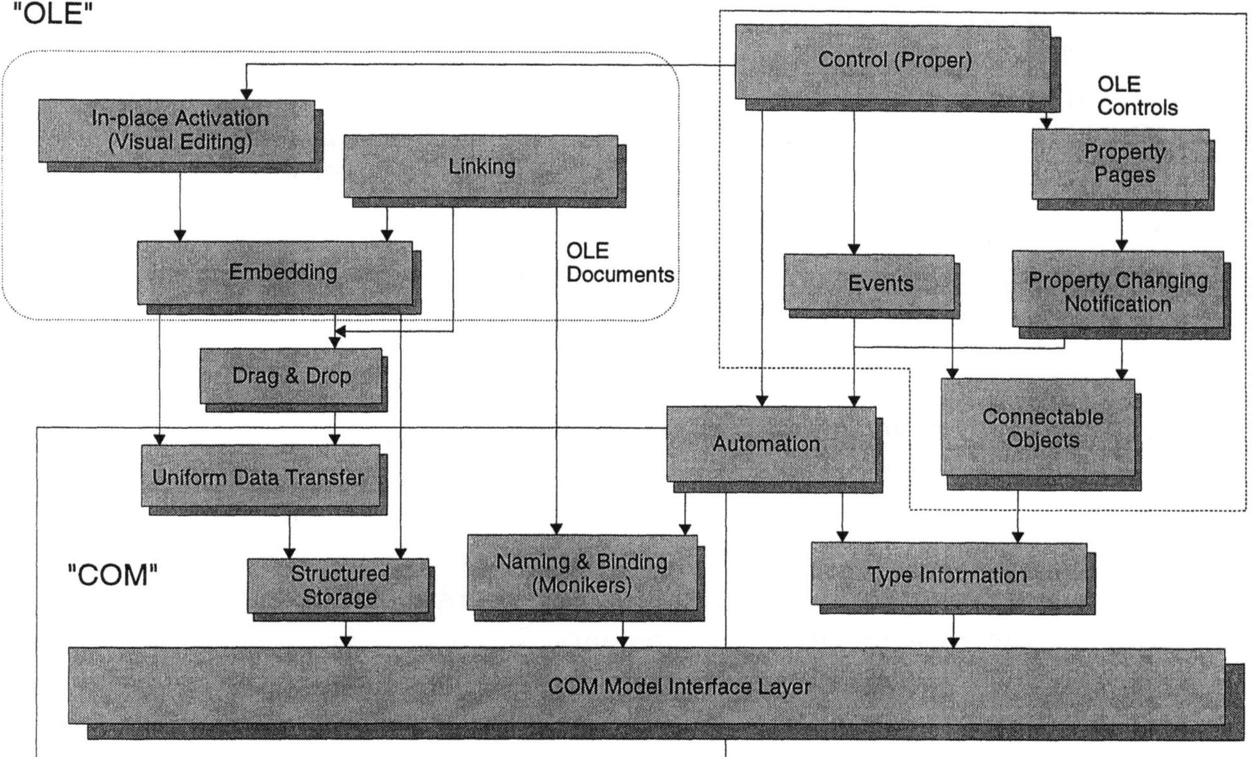


The fundamental goal of COM/OLE 2.x is to allow integration of component objects and applications regardless of the programming language used. By doing so, OLE relieves the application developer and end-users from the responsibility of knowing how to integrate data and applications from diverse sources, thus permitting them to focus on delivering information in a timely manner, and strengthening the competitive position of their employer.

There are a number of important ways OLE 2.x benefits both users and application developers. Through OLE, standard off-the-shelf applications can integrate with each other and with custom applications. For example, a bank's in-house trading application could include an embedded Excel spreadsheet so a user could double click on the spreadsheet when seeking access to it to perform intermediate "what-if" scenarios. The user need not switch applications from the trading application to Excel and try and integrate the results. Likewise, the application developer doesn't have to code spreadsheet functionality into the trading application – they would be able to reuse Excel as if it were an object. The result is more consistent, more intuitive applications.

Additionally, OLE custom controls (OCX) will ensure a large market of third-party add-on products and utilities for standard and customized applications. OCX will supply such widely divergent functionality as advanced "widgets" (GUI elements), telephony support, multimedia, imaging, and more. Because there will be a number of suppliers to select from for each area, developers will be able to select the most appropriate alternative. OCX are reusable component objects and consequently, speed development. Development tools that support OCX will enable application developers to deliver new functionality to their customers. The alternative is to wait until the tool vendor adds the needed functionality or try to code it in-house, if that's possible with the development tools being used.

OLE 2.x allows an organization to use more than one OLE-enabled development environment and still benefit from reusability of code. The reuse in this case is reuse of binary groupings of code rather than reuse of source code as is the case in OOP environments. Because it is difficult for most organizations to uniformly agree on a single development environment, this reuse of binary code solves a large problem for development departments regarding standardization of objects across the organization.

Ultimately, there will likely be changes in the development of applications which parallels the introduction of the assembly line into manufacturing processes. Applications, rather than being large monolithic programs, will consist of collections of cooperating components. Application code, rather than being built from the ground up for each application, will be assembled by defining the interactions of existing and new software components. Some organizations will specialize in the development of components because they can apply specialized knowledge related to the purpose of the component.

This will streamline the process for application assemblers and will enable applications to be delivered more quickly. In addition, applications will be of higher quality. Possibly the most important implication of component-based applications will be the improved responsiveness to required changes over the life of the application. Because a component object is smaller and more autonomous than a traditional application program, changes can be made with less side effects, and the turn-around in quality assurance and distribution is improved. Also, applications composed of component objects will correlate to their real world counterparts more closely and the interpretation of changes in the business model to the source code is more direct and straightforward.

In summary, programs generally exist in one of two states – source code or compiled binary code. OOP applies the benefits of object technology to source code while object-enabled system services such as OLE applies the benefits of object technology to binary code.

OOP languages provide the most productive environment for building OLE component objects because building objects from other objects provides a straightforward and efficient design. When not using an OOP language, one must be concerned with mapping a non-object design to an object design. This will make the source code more complex and cumbersome. Several of the popular 4GL development tools, while trying to emulate an OOP language, suffer from being non-extendible, non-scalable, and proprietary languages.

Despite its widening circle of approval, OLE remains under-developed. For one, it is a difficult technology to master. This is not unusual in the object arena, but some vendors peripheral to the OLE marketplace often infer otherwise.

Another major problem with OLE is its lack of inheritance. As has been stated repeatedly in this report, the properties of inheritance, polymorphism, and encapsulation represent the very essence of object technology. OLE's lack of inheritance is a serious drawback, particularly in the area of code reuse.

Yet another OLE shortcoming is its failure to support OO development, again because of the absence of the inheritance attribute. While OLE components can be modified through aggregation, their capabilities cannot be extended by means of standard OO programming operations.

Microsoft has muddied the waters somewhat by constantly shifting the "vision" for OLE. Ask a group of developers to define OLE and a multitude of different answers will emerge. In its early life, Microsoft presented OLE as an important adjunct to its Office product. Many observers assumed it was inexorably wed to the Office software suite.

OLE's mission has evolved in the last few years. Now, it is as much a communications vehicle as anything else, particularly, says Microsoft, for communication among applications from different vendors. Experience among early users indicates that OLE still works more efficiently in the Office environment than in heterogeneous situations.

Microsoft is diligently working, however, to extend OLE into enterprise operations. To do so, additional services must be added to the OLE model. Some of the newer entities include:

- *OLE Transactions* – addresses the requirements associated with high-end transaction-processing software for security, reliability, and consistency in distributed applications. Microsoft's approach to transaction management provides for scaling desktop and workgroup applications. OLE Transactions also will work with mainstream development tools and desktop productivity applications, taking advantage of the high productivity associated with desktop tools while giving information systems (IS) organizations the ability to add a robust infrastructure in an incremental manner.

- *OLE DB* – enables any type of software that manages data and supports OLE DB interfaces – from desktop spreadsheets to legacy file systems – to participate as a peer of database management systems in an extended "virtual database." Microsoft confirmed its ongoing commitment to support open database connectivity, both as an independent interface to relational database-management systems, and as a subset of OLE DB.

- *Network OLE* – Also called Distributed COM (DCOM) Architecture, allows software components to communicate across a network using industry-standard DCE RPC. A unique feature of Network OLE: This communication is invoked transparent to the components themselves. One set of programming interfaces handles both local and remote communications between components. Existing 32-bit OLE applications are able to take advantage of this new feature without changes. Network OLE also includes an enhanced security model that adds additional application-level security needed in an environment in which users have more freedom to combine data across applications and networks.

- *OLE Team Development* – A set of interfaces that allows OLE components to be managed by repositories, and other tools that support team development and catalog software components and manage them over their life-cycle. The combination of these interfaces and a repository being developed by Microsoft and Texas Instruments provide a development environment in which development tools can integrate with each other and share common components.

Microsoft also has plans to continue to enhance OLE's user productivity features. OLE today allows users to combine data into "compound documents," bringing together data across applications. New interfaces for OLE compound documents will include page-aware layout; irregular shapes; text interfaces for spell-checking, filtering, and indexing; and interfaces to support accessibility tools for the visually impaired.

The third-party software support marketplace has grown tremendously for OLE since its introduction in 1991. Some applications advertise themselves as "OLE-compatible" or "OLE-aware." Unfortunately, this is an incomplete description because two such applications may support completely different OLE features. This might prevent them from being interoperable despite their proclaimed relationship with OLE.

Basic OLE features include:

- Linking and embedding

- Visual editing

- Automation – as a client, controlling other OLE objects; and as a server, providing OLE objects for others to control

- OLE controls

- OLE type library support and browser

Linking and embedding, which have been OLE capabilities since its inception, enable the formation of compound documents such as a Microsoft Word document with Excel spreadsheets (or parts of them) inside it. Fundamentally, the containing document acts as a host for any number of linked or embedded documents.

This host document need not know how to format the guest application; instead, the guest application must provide formatting for the host document through the OLE interface. Without such an interoperability standard, developers and users would find it difficult to combine charts, documents, and pictures from a variety of tools into a single, cohesive document.

To decide whether to embed or link, these guidelines are often used:

- *Linking* – keeps a relative pointer to a file that contains the guest application's data. Changes made by anyone who uses the linked file will be reflected in the container, but the linked file must be moved with the container or the link will be broken.

- *Embedding* – keeps the guest application's data within the host. This data travels with the host application, but changes to the embedded file are not reflected outside of the host environment.

Visual editing is an extension of linking and embedding where there is a tightly-knit or cooperative relationship between host and guest applications. With visual editing, the guest temporarily takes over the host application to deliver control of the guest application to the user.

When visual editing is performed correctly, the user needs little or no knowledge of the fact that control is switched from the host application to the guest application. Visual editing is performed in place and as such prevents the confusing interfaces sometimes associated with linking and embedding without visual editing support. Rather than windows appearing suddenly on the user's screen, the guest application opens seamlessly inside the host window. Toolbars and menus can be shared so they have functions of both host and guest available to the user.

OLE components intermixed by linking and embedding with visual editing can provide a common appearance to an application. But this common appearance comes with a price: The developer has little control over the objects. The objects react to user operations, but they are not under the control of the host application. For example, if a chart is embedded in a word processing document, the user can double click the chart to edit it in place. However, such ability on the user's part does not mean that the word processor can programmatically control the chart. OLE Automation describes this kind of programmatic control over OLE components. An application or DLL that exposes these OLE components is called an OLE automation server.

The programmer of an OLE automation server determines which properties and methods within the solution are to be exposed to others through OLE automation. Other private objects are invisible to external users. To use an automation server, programmers need to know only the name of the application containing the object, the object's class name, and the name of the property or method the programmer wants to use.

OLE controls extend the capabilities of the software development environment. The extended capabilities follow the standards used by automation servers with respect to properties and methods and also support foreign events. This feature provides the host application with notification that an event has occurred in the guest application. For example, when an OLE control provides a grid for data preview, and the user selects cells in the grid, it causes an event in the host to initiate indicating which cell was clicked. Therefore, programmers write code to respond to such an event.

An OLE control is similar to a DLL except that an OLE control resides in a controlled environment and a DLL does not. Another difference is that unlike a DLL, an OLE control does not require that the user know the details of calling sequences or structure, they can simply be browsed by an object browser.

Unlike DLLs, OLE servers use type libraries as a standard way to document the properties and methods contained within. Along with a standard help file, type libraries provide a catalog of OLE objects. With a browser, programmers can view the list of available objects as well as the exposed features of each object for use in applications.

Most browsers also provide a paste button that enables programmers to paste the selected property or method into their code. In turn, they can look for objects providing the needed functionality and then integrate them into their code. The type library resembles a C header file except that it comes in a standard, easy-to-read format that ties into online help. The type library also is accessible to those who select its related object from the registry.

When selecting a development tool for programming with OLE objects, programmers should consider whether the tool will support :

- Linking or embedding OLE objects

- In-place editing of embedded OLE objects

- Programmatic control of embedded OLE objects

- Creation of an in-process OLE server (an application that provides objects)

- Creation of an out-of-process OLE server

- Automation of an OLE object

- Hosting of an OLE control

- Creation of an OLE control

- Integration and browsing of OLE type libraries

If the tool does not support such activities, programmers should consider whether the features it does support are sufficient for current and future development needs. Programmers also should ask whether the tool fits into the long-term strategy of their group and their company.

## Other Methodologies

First and foremost among "other methodologies" is OpenDoc. It emanates from a consortium of vendors and is designed to run in a wide variety of environments as illustrated in Figure 9.4. OpenDoc components can be used to build compound documents, custom applications, and C/S applications, all based on CORBA standards. Whether it be OS/2, UNIX or Windows, OpenDoc is amenable to diverse configurations.

### Figure 9.4 OpenDoc Architecture

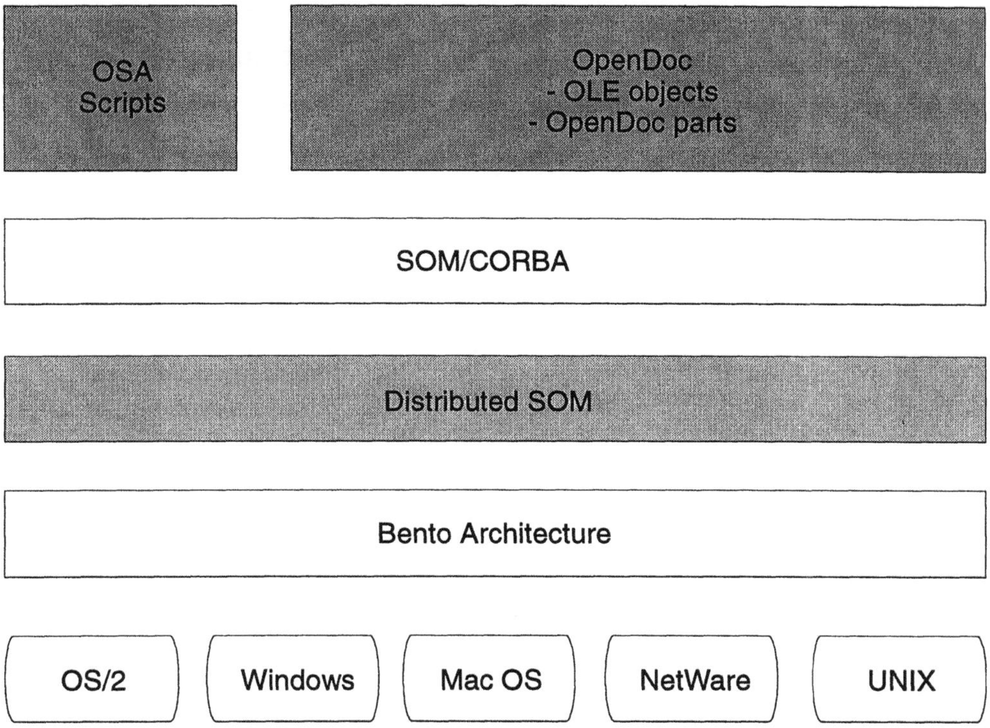

In the views of their own respective creators, OLE is application-centric, OpenDoc by contrast is content-centric. In addition to this fundamental differentiation, the OpenDoc consortium pledged compliance with the OMG's CORBA standards. Microsoft, on the other hand, has backed and filled on the topic of CORBA. First for it, then ignoring it, they have been inconsistent in terms of CORBA and related standards.

As depicted in Figure 9.4, OpenDoc has multiple architectural components:

1. *SOM* – A programming framework for creating, packaging, and manipulating binary libraries developed by IBM for OS/2 configurations

2. *DSOM* – A dynamic linking capability that enables objects to communicate across diverse operating systems, networks, and applications

3. *Bento* – A portable object storage library which allows OpenDoc to save and exchange compound, multiple documents

4. *Open Scripting Architecture (OSA)* – A standard that enables multiple scripting languages to coexist. It is an API that supports workflow and application-independent scripting

Some of the major advantages of OpenDoc include:

- It supports inheritance, unlike its OLE 2.x counterpart

- Its interface is easier than OLE's rather complicated mechanism

- It requires fewer API calls than OLE

- It is not an integral part of the Windows monolith such as is the case with OLE, OpenDoc is designed for cross-platform applications.

OpenDoc's weaknesses center on its lack of strong third-party support. OLE has widespread support among these vendors. In addition, only a few development tools target the OpenDoc technology. This is changing, but the question remains as to whether it is changing fast enough.

OpenDoc supports OLE 2.x by encapsulating OLE components within OpenDoc components. The building blocks of OpenDoc are portrayed in Figure 9.5.

## Figure 9.5 OpenDoc Building Blocks

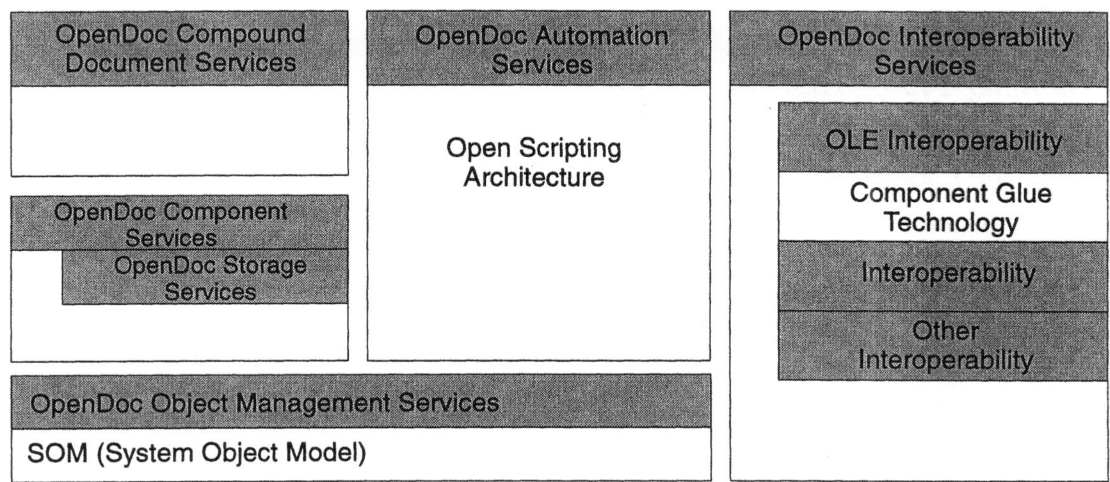


Perhaps the most visible example of the frustration encountered by object technology adherents is in the twisted fate of the "Taligent Adventure." Finally dissolved in 1995, Taligent's odyssey is representative of so many ambitious pioneering efforts in the field of technology or as it is sometimes referred to: "the field of dreams." Taligent's Adventure proceeds as follows:

- *Late 1980s* – Apple began work on an OO OS called Pink.

- *October 1991* – IBM and Apple agreed to launch a joint venture based on Pink. The initial goal was to develop system software and tools for the nascent PowerPC platform and for other processors.

- *Early 1992* – IBM and Apple formally created a separate development company named Taligent to carry forward the work on object technology.

- *1993* – Taligent canceled its work on OS creation. It vowed instead to focus on frameworks based on C++. These frameworks were to be used in building collaborative applications able to run on diverse platforms and operating systems.

- *January 1994* – HP bought into the Taligent effort.

- *Early 1995* – A beta release of Taligent's CommonPoint system was released.

- *Summer 1995* – IBM shipped CommonPoint for the AIX platform.

- *December 1995* – Taligent no longer exists. The organizational structure of Taligent is folded. IBM, Apple, and HP retain licensing rights to the technology. IBM vows to provide ongoing development of the CommonPoint package.

The end result of this adventure was a valuable framework called CommonPoint, whose future at present is uncertain. There certainly was no OO OS, which is how the project began. Ultimately, there was no Taligent either. All of this illustrates the perils of new technology and also the underlying complexity of object technology.

OO OS complexity can be seen in Figure 9.6. In a "pure" implementation of the OO OS, everything above the kernel is a replaceable object. Files are replaced by the reality of persistent objects that are transparently moved between memory and mass storage.

## Figure 9.6 Object-Oriented Operating System

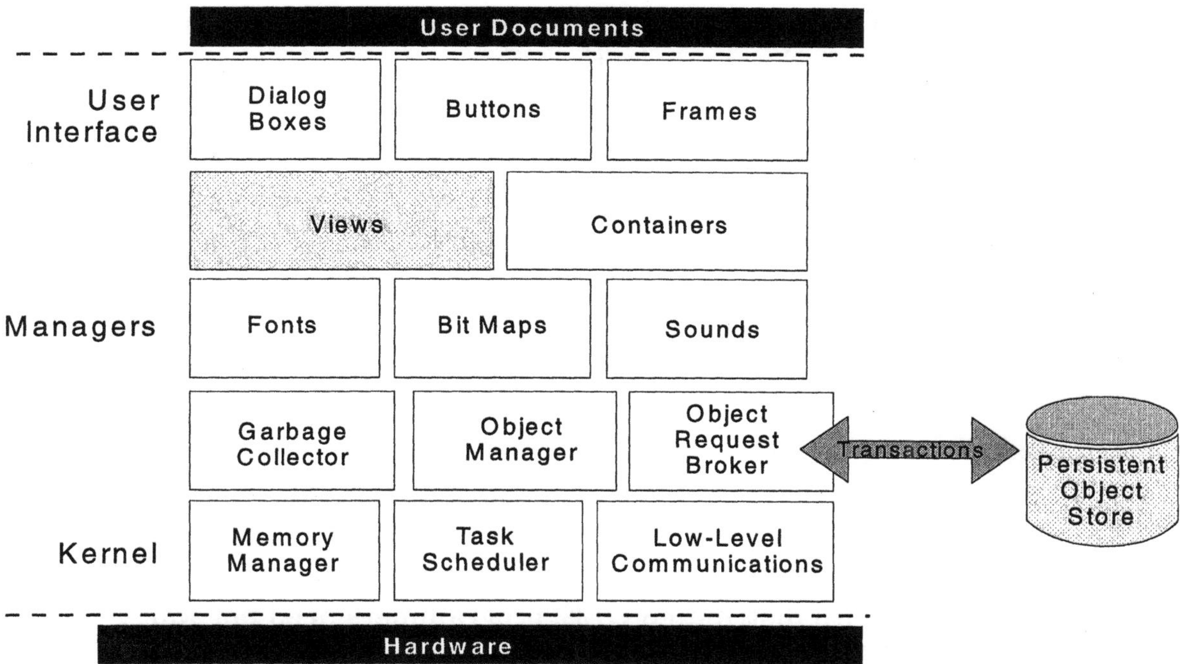


NextStep is probably closer to the generic OO OS model portrayed in Figure 9.6, at least among products in general distribution. It is built on the public domain Mach kernel.

IBM's OS/2 Warp is OO to a degree. Its WorkPlace Shell user interface offers an object hierarchy which is accessible to developers.

## Future Trends

OLE, CORBA, OpenDoc, and related technologies will weigh heavily in future advances in the world of objects. All of these mechanisms can claim some degree of standardization, whether it be de facto or de jure in nature.

All OLE features, for example, are implemented on top of COM, the Microsoft object technology. COM provides the linkage that enables interaction between an OLE client (known as the container application) and an OLE server (the application providing the objects). COM supports OLE access on one PC.

An extension to this technology is the DCOM which enables two OLE-aware applications operating on different PCs to communicate with each other across a network. This change from COM to DCOM is transparent to the OLE object and is handled entirely by the OS.

Distributed OLE applications will significantly change the way people think about computer applications. Consider a personnel application running on a PC that communicates through OLE with an employee object running on another PC on the same network. The employee object may be supporting many applications, each running on different PCs. It may use other OLE applications, which in turn may run on still other PCs.

Distributed OLE enables the division of processing, the use of networks as they were intended, load balancing, and centralized control. With distributed OLE, multitier C/S applications are more easily implemented. OLE technology permits the pieces of an application to run on different machines in a standard way. With distributed OLE, programmers need not worry about where the pieces of their solution are running and instead can concentrate on the logic of their solutions.

Taking the ideal of distributed technology one step further, the Internet could provide a very large selection of possible remote objects. Such issues as security, performance, and licensing will need to be carefully considered in such a dynamic environment.

Both Microsoft and the OMG are fighting spiritedly to gain ascendancy in the Internet sphere. They both hope to make their respective architectures serve as a model for transferring objects across the Internet.

On another front, Microsoft's OO successor to Windows NT, known as Cairo, is in its pre-release stage. It employs a unique object file system which turns the entire mass storage unit into a logically unified document file that reveals its internal objects to the user.

Whether the significant technical upheaval generated by Cairo will find widespread acceptance within the user community remains to be seen. It may be that Cairo, much like NT itself, will take several years to gain a foothold.

On the other hand, Microsoft has proven to be particularly adept at building market demand for their products.

# Chapter 10

# Performance Issues

## General Principles

There are an infinite variety of issues affecting performance in OO systems, much of them centered on the architectural design of the system being measured. One of the current problems emanating from object technology itself is the issue of granularity; objects are constructed on too low a level of detail.

Rather than having an object or class of objects that manages an identifiable functional action, there often are an endless series of micro-steps, which perform minute operations that ultimately contribute to a recognizable function. A developer working with this myopic level of detail, however, loses valuable time sorting out such object minutiae.

Thus, low-level objects not only do not reduce complexity, they become another part of the overall development problem. The numerous low-level objects that comprise an accounts receivable object, for example, typically invoke hundreds of detailed methods. Ultimately, all of these methods contribute to the few major objects that make up an accounts receivable function. A developer should be able to work with those few major objects, not endless quantities of so-called micro objects.

It is vital that developers remove themselves from the "swamp of detail" represented by low-level objects. Rather than laboring to create enterprise applications utilizing hundreds of micro objects, developers need to ascend to a higher level of abstraction, one that allows them to manage objects that represent recognizable functions within the enterprise.

One of the methods used to improve developer productivity and performance is to create business objects. The latter are high-level objects that represent aggregations of low-level objects. Conceptually, these business objects behave as single objects. This means developers only need to interface with a few methods rather than a multitude of the low-level variety.

Business objects solve many of the problems of working with objects:

- They render objects easy to reuse because developers can quickly grasp what the object is and does.

- They reduce complexity by encapsulating all low-level objects that comprise the business object and their internal workings. Therefore, the developer does not see them or need to manage them.

- They speed the learning curve by allowing developers who are learning object technology to work naturally with objects that resemble the familiar business entities being modeled.

From an organizational perspective, the end result is that developers and business people can work together, interactively, on an application because the development environment provides a common high-level vocabulary. Rather than abstracting business rules to procedural code, developers can work at a higher level with objects that are consistent with how people perceive their business. Performance and quality are thus enhanced.

The OMG has worked to define business objects in multiple ways. One workgroup has created a library of common business objects such as those that can be applied across different industries. Other workgroups have focused on vertical markets. The vertical market involves objects that can be used in particular business sectors such as banking, communications, and manufacturing.

Several industry pioneers have built business objects for specific purposes, often using multiple object technologies to reach their goal. Among the tools employed to create these objects are IBM's SOM, Digital's ObjectBroker, Iona's Orbix, and Microsoft's OLE. Except for Microsoft's OLE, all are CORBA-compliant products.

In the OMG effort, objects are divided into four categories (see Table 10.1). Each of the four include facilities that can be adapted to CORBA. Participants among the various OMG domain task forces believe that their work will bolster the opportunities for software reuse.

### Table 10.1 Business Objects for Financial Systems

| Business Support | ◆ Accounting |
| | ◆ Credit and Funds Transfer |
| | ◆ Settlement |
| | ◆ Statutory Compliance |
| **Customer Support** | ◆ Alternate Distribution |
| | ◆ Customer Descriptions |
| | ◆ Online Banking |
| **Decision Support** | ◆ Channel Management |
| | ◆ Contract Management |
| | ◆ Relationship Management |
| **Financial Products** | ◆ Insurance |
| | ◆ Financial Instrument Trades |
| | ◆ Portfolio Management |
| | ◆ Product Definitions |
| | ◆ Negotiated Agreements |

In the world of database systems, objects present some unique performance problems. Whereas rows in a table – as found in a RDBMS – are closely linked physically, such is not the case in an OODBMS. The latter allows objects to be dispersed in a flexible manner.

Such flexibility has its advantages and disadvantages. On one hand, the database can be structured in a very dynamic fashion. On the other hand, performance can deteriorate when groups of objects are accessed.

Several approaches are available to minimize performance degradation caused by object dispersal, but one of the most widely used is clustering. This involves locating object classes and aggregations closely together on disk in order reduce access time. Clustering is nothing more than creating logical associations among otherwise independent objects.

## Performance Variables

Many of the variables affecting performance have to do with organizing, accessing, and transferring data. This is true whether managing object-based systems or not. Benchmarks are often used to measure performance, but they must obviously reflect the parameters by which they were constructed. If a benchmark was built to test just a few aspects of system operation, then a sense of overall performance will not be achieved.

Organization of the database is a key component of performance. Some of the major issues in this area include:

- *Impact on Network Traffic Due to Queries* – Distributed architectures feature large amounts of traffic transmitted between clients and servers. This can generate severe performance problems. Solutions include efficient management of user queries, stored methods in a server to perform intermediate processing without creating additional network traffic, and replicating objects (with their accompanying data) over multiple servers.

- *Database Organization* – The structure of object lists (comparable to indexes in relational systems) determines how data will be accessed which has a major impact on performance.

- *Disk Organization* – The physical location of objects on multiple disks directly influences system performance. As mentioned earlier, clustering is an effective remedy for poorly performing object database applications.

- *Dynamic Monitoring of Database Performance* – Monitoring tools can be helpful in identifying problem areas. Tools will provide information such as quantity of searches through an object class, number of disk accesses required for each category of data access, types of data accesses being used, and network organization of most commonly accessed object classes.

## Database Factors

As described earlier, clustering is an important technique when database performance is an issue. Such clustering can be organized by class hierarchy or by other relationships among objects.

Another performance enhancer is initiation of one or more cache repositories for more efficient access. There are endless cache schemes, most targeted to a particular set of operating conditions. The ultimate goal of all databases is to gather objects as close as possible to their point of use.

Clustering, caching, and assorted other performance-enhancing techniques are extremely useful methodologies when seeking to improve system response. A larger concern in this area, however, is architectural in nature.

OODBMSs have architectures that are fundamentally different than those of conventional RDBMSs. The nature of this difference is illustrated in Figure 10.1. As shown in the figure, both the RDBMS and the OODBMS have C/S architectures (components of the DBMS are shaded). The difference is in the division of labor between client and server.

## Figure 10.1 Database Management System Architectures

**Relational**

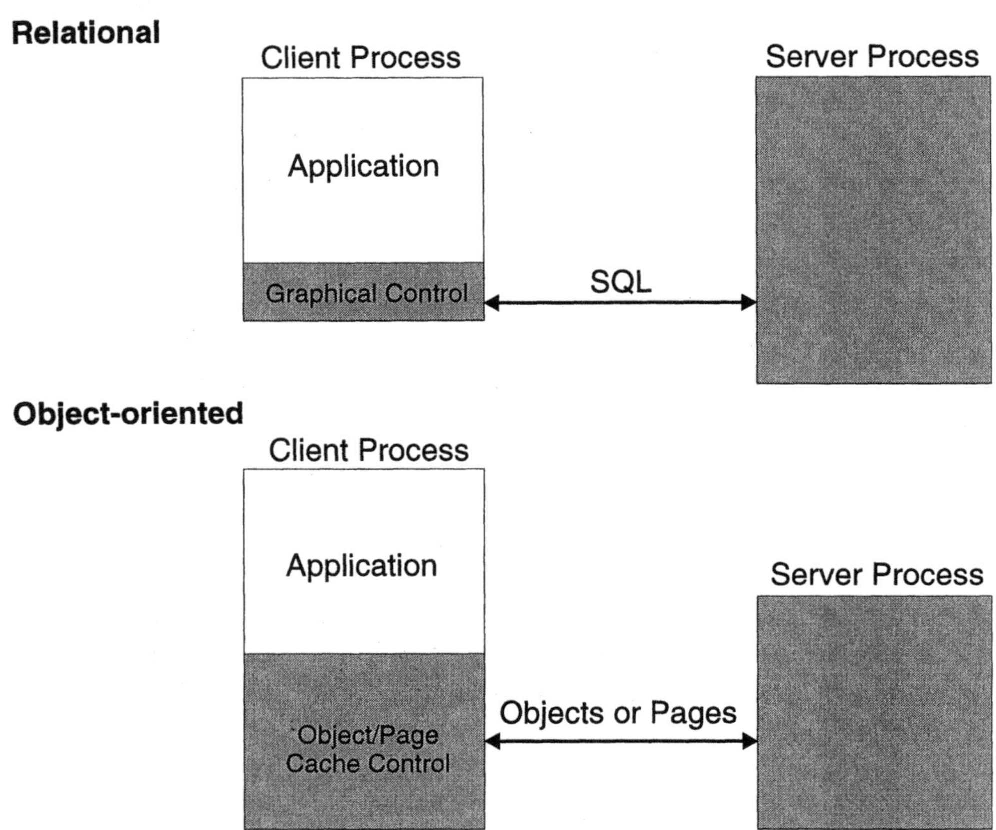


In a conventional relational system, the architecture is designed for applications to send SQL queries to the server. All query processing is done in the server, which returns data satisfying the query to the client. The server also handles transaction processing and recovery. The client's responsibility is to manage application processing, together with managing cursors that allow the application to range over the data returned by the query.

This architecture avoids network traffic because only rows explicitly required by the application are returned from the server. This architecture also is a good idea if the server is extremely powerful compared to the clients (for example, when servers are mainframes, and clients are PCs with relatively less memory and computational power).

In a typical OODBMS architecture, the client plays a much greater role. These architectures are based on what is sometimes called a data-shipping approach. In this approach, data is shipped from servers to clients so much of the OODBMS's processing (including query processing) and application processing is performed at the client.

This provides two advantages. The data-shipping approach moves the data closer to the application and supports efficient fine-grained interleaving between application processing and access to the next persistent object (found by following a pointer) required by the application. The second advantage is that DBMS functions are off-loaded from the server to the clients. This allows a given server to support many more clients and takes maximum advantage of the resources of the typically numerous clients on the network. The difference in architecture creates an enormous performance advantage for OODBMS over RDBMS in most OODBMS applications.

## Object Design Factors

One of the major factors in the future success of object technology hinges on the techniques used to distribute and execute remote objects. Certainly an important player in this regard is Microsoft and its Cairo OS which upgrades their older NT package.

Cairo's specific technology capabilities have been evolving, but distributing and executing remote objects is a fundamental feature of its offerings. Microsoft's Visual Basic 4.x software development tool contained remote object handling routines long before Cairo was released. These same features have been incorporated into Cairo.

When the Enterprise Edition of Visual Basic is installed on a client platform, an OLE Automation proxy is added to the mix (see Figure 10.2). A Window Registry module keeps track as to whether objects are located on a local or remote system. Thus, when an OLE client seeks to access an object, the Window Registry knows where to locate it.

## Figure 10.2 Remote Object Processing

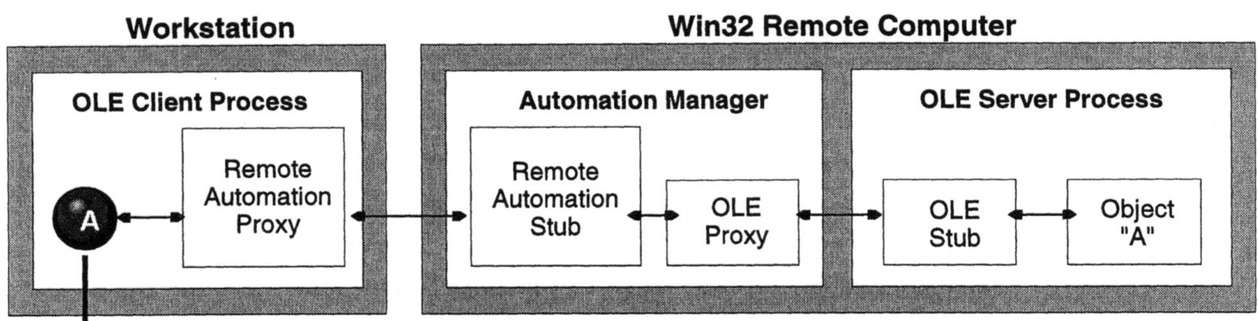


If the desired object is on a remote system, the Registry communicates with the OLE proxy. The latter converts the OLE automation call to a Windows NT (in the Visual Basic environment) RPC. The object is then transmitted across the network, where it is received by an automation manager. The automation manager, which resides on a server, is a Visual Basic module that is multithreaded and distributable.

The automation manager receives the RPC-generated data flow and converts it to OLE automation calls, which are then forwarded to the server application. Both the client and server interface solely with OLE automation initiatives, not RPC directives.

In the Visual Basic world, performance with remote object technology can be problematic. Each object occupies about 500 KB of RAM. Therefore, running multiple remote servers simultaneously can seriously impact system response time.

Within Visual Basic, two types of OLE automation servers are possible. There is an in-process server and an out-of-process server. A server is code that manages objects. An in-process server has code execute on client (for example, a dynamic link library [DLL]). An out-of-process server runs on a remote system to manage remote objects or int the same system, but in a different process. Both types expose methods and properties that can be browsed by all OLE client applications.

In-process servers are implemented as DLLs and run in the same client process that accesses it. Out-of-process servers have their own address space. They require the service arrangements portrayed in Figure 10.1. Visual

Basic's Enterprise Edition allows these out-of-process servers to be executed remotely over a network.

# Chapter 11

# Object-Oriented Implementation Plan

## General Principles

There are four definable steps on the road to OO systems. There is OO analysis, design, development, and on-going software management.

OO analysis involves a fundamental shift in an organization's approach to system conceptualization. As opposed to older methods that focus on individual procedures and the data that accompanies them, OO analysis looks at problem solving from the viewpoint of larger, more cohesive, self-contained modules. Each of these modules must reinforce the guiding principles of object technology enumerated repeatedly in this report: inheritance, encapsulation, and polymorphism.

The analysis phase must also think of the "big picture." In other words, do not attack a new project in a tactical sense, but approach it strategically. This means that solutions should tend to be less specific to the problem at hand (although certainly that problem must be addressed), but more directed to an enterprisewide, generic outcome.

By dispensing with conventional, parochial approaches to problem analysis, object technology implementors can lay the groundwork for wider benefits to accrue from a specific system solution. This occurs because analysts are thinking on two levels. One is to solve the problem at hand. The second is to create libraries of generic objects capable of further use while addressing that immediate problem.

In the current procedural approach to system development, hands-on programming and testing occupy more than two-thirds of a project team's time. With object technology, more time is spent in the analysis phase. Perhaps more than one-third of the overall project's allotted time will be spent on analysis. Conversely, the programming and testing time commitment will be reduced.

As a result, objects can more accurately reflect the continuing flow of business activity than earlier methodologies. To exploit this capability, however, analysts must become intimately familiar with such business activity; they must spend more time analyzing.

OO design introduces a different approach to problem solution than the familiar waterfall technique, which has become so familiar to technology implementors over the years. This new approach emphasizes reiteration and cycles rather than discrete, measured steps evidenced in older methods.

Most designers are familiar with the so-called waterfall technique, whereby a project has clearly definable (although somewhat artificial) steps that include problem identification, design, code and test, implementation, and maintenance. The concept involved here is that once a step is completed, it is almost never visited again. Maintenance, of course, is the sole exception to this concept.

The ideal state of OO design, not always achieved, is to revisit one or more of the design steps throughout a project's life. This is important because new information is always becoming available which can help to redefine previous solution techniques. The entire process is viewed as a continuing cycle rather than discrete, "now-it-is-over" steps.

OO development requires the selection of tools and support routines that will aid the overall effort. Among these support routines will be code generators, object creation utilities, object library browsers, test modules to verify application viability, and a multitude of related software tools.

There is no single tool or family of tools that meets the complete needs of system developers. There are, however, products that offer partial solutions and these must be chosen with great care. Due to the relative immaturity of the object tool market, many of the tools selected now will be replaced by more robust offerings in the years ahead.

OO management is comprised of all the steps associated with assuring future reuse of object classes that are germane to an entire enterprise, and perhaps to an entire industry. To achieve this goal, an object repository must be created which categorizes and stores objects that have universal appeal.

The object repository, along with its operating rules, becomes an important source for future development. It will grow in importance and complexity over time, enough so an object repository manager may be appointed to control this vital resource. This is not unlike the role of a database manager found in RDBMS installations.

As with any complex initiative, there are standard rules that accompany the move toward object technology. Many of these rules are, in actuality, applicable to any emerging technology and include:

- An individual high up in the organizational hierarchy should be given overall control of object technology initiatives. This person should be both knowledgeable and have sufficient clout to influence events.

- Develop a promotional strategy to combat the naysayers. Append the object task if possible to some other new project which has already gained widespread support, sort of a "Trojan Horse" approach.

- Present a strategic plan to management of short, intermediate, and long term goals relative to current and future applications. Within this strategic plan, expound on the people and technology needed to accomplish the task.

  It is necessary to have a cadre of "object warriors" in-house ready to launch high profile object migrations. Object technology is difficult to master and veteran employees may resist change, so create this "elite unit" from whatever departments and offices are able to supply members.

- Develop a broad transition plan for the organization. Within this plan identify all the supporting technologies (network capacities, development methodologies, and so forth) that will form part of the transition plan.

Once OO projects are launched, it is vital to schedule regular program reviews. In these reviews, technology proponents must explain and justify all development decisions to functional users and other technologists. This exercise instills discipline and rigor to the implementation process, a type of "trial by your peers."

The old proverb, "Let a thousand flowers bloom," can be applied. Multiple OO project teams should be built over time, always insuring to leverage past gains and experience levels.

## Client/Server Case Study

Certainly one of the most important architectural advances in this decade is that of C/S. It is becoming the most prominent example of distributed computing in the marketplace today.

C/S, as with almost any other technology, can benefit from OO analysis, design, and implementation. Current C/S architectures are moving toward a multitier configuration. The older two-tier design featuring server, client, and network is being expanded to feature specialized servers. A typical example of the older design is the growing presence of application servers in a multitier approach.

When evaluating the use of object technology in C/S environments, the focus naturally turns to Microsoft. Not that their effort is necessarily superior to others, but their use of the ubiquitous OLE package in many settings has gained the attention of the entire industry.

Multitier architecture offers an efficient way to develop C/S business solutions. It is technology-neutral and can be implemented on any system that enables standard interfaces for each of the logical levels called "tiers." With an emphasis on discrete interfaces between tiers, implementation details are hidden from users. The functionality of each tier, called components, can be written in different languages and maintained independently. This capacity allows the developer to use multiple tools to get the job done quickly and correctly.

A C/S business solution is generally defined as an application distributed between a client platform and a server platform, connected over a network. In reality, however, a C/S solution does not have to be thought of in terms of physical processors and networks. It is the business solution that is divided into distinct parts – a logical rather than physical model for C/S computing. The parts or smallest units of functionality called "services," can run on any physical machine or even share the same processor. Movement of services, assuming availability of resources, between physical machines is a performance issue and should not affect the functionality of the service. This concept of multitier partitioning running on a single machine or over many machines in a distributed environment is fundamental to designing C/S solutions.

People generally organize large, complex tasks into smaller, simpler ones to reach their goals more easily. By breaking down a complex job into a series of smaller tasks, risk is reduced, clarity is enhanced, and cost is moderated. Business-solution development is no exception. Dividing a large computer business solution into many smaller tasks also reduces the risk, cost, and time of development and facilitates maintenance. C/S multitier architecture allows for the decomposition of a complex business problem into discrete services that a workable solution must deliver. The multitier developer is able to concentrate more on the delivery of these services.

### Standard Interfaces

The rationale for a standard interface: Any business solution that can interoperate with the interface, and has permission, can use it. This concept is important to the future of C/S development. If C/S computing is to be successful, it must have better and faster methods of enabling business solutions. A solution can enable any available business object it needs to provide needed functionality and business rules.

Programming is in the process of changing drastically. As use of component interfaces becomes standard operating procedure and more components become available, solution builders worry less about issues such as memory management and graphics generation and more about solving business problems. They engage the components and services needed to complete the business task at hand.

Development languages are changing to support this concept and to provide easier ways to create business solutions from a combination of commercial and custom-developed components. The fundamental Microsoft enabling technology for these interfaces is OLE. For it is OLE components that encapsulate functionality and provide entry points to that functionality through OLE-based interfaces. This allows access to the component from within any OLE-based language. Therefore, developers at multiple experience levels can choose the tools most appropriate for them, yet share the same set of reusable components.

## Multitier Design

A multitier design allows developers to fragment complex business processes into smaller pieces, allowing for reusability. The simplest form of a multitier model is the three-tier model. The three-tier model clearly reflects C/S architecture principles. It uses a services model that consists of:

- *User-Services Tier* – The front-end client that communicates with the user through a GUI. Client code at this level calls upon the available business-services level to provide encapsulated business functionality.

- *Business-Services Tier* – A collection of services that enforce business rules, process information, and manage transactions.

- *Data-Services Tier* – A collection of decision-independent data used by the business-services level to make decisions. This can be a database management system stored on a mainframe or accessed from a data service on the Internet.

The three-tier model can be extended in several ways:

- Add a new service to the business-services level and modify the user-services level to use it

- Add new data to the data-services level

- Modify an existing service to improve its capabilities

- Add a new solution to the user-services level that uses the business-services level in new ways

The three-tier approach elevates the definition of services from instructions and application programming interface (API) calls to business services. A service is a logical business function that can be aggregated into physical code called a component. These components are referred to as business objects. The developer's job becomes that of combining these business components into a solution.

The collection of business components can be thought of as a set of business-service relationships. By grouping these business components in different ways, different business solutions are provided. Business components can be called by other business components in the same tier or at higher tiers. These business components expose these capabilities:

- *Properties* – The characteristics of the business object. For example, in a tax-calculation service, properties might include Social Security Number and Marital Status

- *Methods* – The functionality implemented such as Calculate Tax Bracket or Compute Tax Liability

- *Events* – The notification of the occurrence of an event to the caller (the client) of the business object

In this design, a business object can function logically as both a client and a server. It can be called by another business object and it can call upon other business objects to complete its tasks. The critical characteristic of a business object is that it encapsulates its details and hides them from a user. Only the interface is important to that user in terms of access.

## Tier Categories

The user-services tier is the direct interface between a user and the computer. It provides a familiar set of interfaces that display, edit, and accept data. A user interface should have an intuitive way of entering data, calling upon business objects to act on that data, and presenting results back to the user in an informative manner.

The user-services tier then makes various calls to the business-services tier to act upon data and to request business objects in an efficient manner. This tier is more concerned with providing and presenting users with solutions to business problems than with details of the way in which the problem was solved.

The business-services tier encapsulates business rules and processes providing clarity of purpose for each individual object. Business components are mixed with many other components at this level. Various business solutions can share a set of business objects and call upon one or more of these business components, usually through the user-services tier, to provide a solution.

Initially, three-tier C/S development requires building business objects at the business-services tier, in addition to building solutions at the user-services tier. After several business solutions are built, a solid set of business objects will exist that represent the user's enterprise computing environment. Thereafter, development of new business solutions may require no new business objects or very few.

Building business components can be a complex task requiring a thorough understanding of a user's overall business, and how various segments of the user's business interact with a common business object. For instance, businesses have customers, and most segments of a business interact with customer information in some way. As a result, it makes sense to build a customer component that is reusable across the company. To do so, and to eliminate redundant customer databases, a user must understand how various departments interact with customer information, what information they manage, and what existing manual processes might be automated by this component.

As a core set of business components becomes available, development takes on a more economical pace, and the components themselves become a rapid business-solution environment. A new solution then requires the linking of business services with data and presentation. Business components can be added to create new solution functionality.

These are important rules for three-tier development:

- Build a business object only once. Never build two business objects that perform identical tasks

- Buy third-party business objects when possible, and build only as a last resort

Creating business components requires a more rigorous, technical approach than building solutions out of components. It is important to have experience modeling business processes and data, in addition to having an understanding of OO modeling techniques. The tools a user chooses to build business components also are often more technical.

Traditionally, data business objects are thought of in terms of databases. The data-services tier actually consists of data in any form:

- *Databases* – This aspect of data business objects is well understood today. Databases implement security and data business objects well. Typically, databases are called by several different business solutions for similar data, which causes each business solution to have similar code to work with the data. The data-services tier should not be called directly by a business solution at the user-services tier, which would result in a two-tier model. Instead, a database activity should be initiated by a business object in the business-services tier.

- *Mainframes* – Mainframe databases can be accessed in a way similar to any database through an ODBC driver and gateway. Mainframe processes that create or calculate data can be defined by technologies such as LU 6.2 and then called from the business-services tier to act as a data-services tier component.

- *Internet* – Like mainframes, the Internet provides a large collection of data business objects that can be used by the business-services tier.

# Guiding Principles

Once a decision is made to adopt object technology within an organization, whether in whole or part, numerous issues will need to be addressed to achieve success. In addition to specific questions and issues, a general strategy for implementation must be developed. This strategy will be comprised of a series of goals and milestones such as:

- Appropriate staff and management personnel need to receive training appropriate to their job responsibilities. Obviously those programmers will need more intense tutoring than those at a management level.

- An initial implementation plan must be created with accompanying milestones. This will allow progress to be measured, although the plan will undoubtedly go through numerous alterations as the work unfolds.

- A test project must be selected. As with any new technology launch, this project must be selected with care. It should represent a visible application, but not mission-critical in nature. Selecting too obscure a task will fail to bring plaudits and critical future support.

- Specific analysis, design, and development methodologies will be chosen based on the nature of the project, amount of funding available, and number of skilled practitioners able to work on it. On a maiden voyage through the "wilds of object technology," it makes good sense to bring in outside expertise if the budget can support such a move. It is important, however, to not allow an outside consultant to become entrenched. When the project is completed, the consultant should move on.

- When the system is implemented, all considerations relating to interaction with legacy systems must have been finalized.

- Iteration is the name of the game. Design, development, and implementation tasks must be revisited continuously. Lessons learned will be applied to all succeeding projects.

Perhaps the most vital issues when adopting object technology (or any new technology) is accommodation for legacy systems. The object wrapper approach is most commonly used to accomplish this. Wrapping means nothing more than treating the legacy system as one large object.

Each of the legacy system's services is defined as a method for that object. Typically, special software is written which encompasses the legacy system to translate method requests into calls that will be understandable to that legacy system. This software is often quite complex and requires experienced implementors.

# Chapter 12

# Future Trends

## Software Tools and Practices

What are some of the software tools that will come to the forefront in the immediate years ahead? The list is quite extensive. Some tools are fairly popular already, others are barely visible to market analysts Several tools were covered in detail earlier in this report such as CORBA and activeX

One technology offering that should a great leap in popularity is OpenDoc. This OO component model can take existing code and wrap it in OpenDoc then store it in a class library for later use. An operation such as this may prove to be the breakthrough technique that software reuse has been waiting for.

When discussing objects, reuse is always one of the first virtues cited by its advocates. In actual practice, however, software reuse has achieved limited success to this point. One of the reasons for this is the time and effort needed to generate a viable reuse policy. Developers cannot always afford to do the administrative and technical things necessary to guarantee an effective software reuse activity within an organization.

OpenDoc was not created solely to support reuse, but that may ultimately become its most important legacy. This is not to demean its multiplatform versatility and inherent openness, but OpenDoc's biggest contribution may lay in its orderly support for reuse.

"Give me your tired, your poor, your dispossessed" says the old adage. To Smalltalk and some C++ adherents, this plea applies to those COBOL addicts who are heartily trumpeting the object COBOL products now appearing on the market. These products almost universally claim compliance with the ANSI standard for object COBOL.

Yes, COBOL may be old, but the object version is another offering that can give an improvement to object technology. As with OpenDoc, its primary benefit may be in aiding software reuse.

Object COBOL provides the capability to embed existing COBOL routines in an object wrapper and make it, for example, an OLE-type object. The difficulty in producing object wrapper software, however is that it is moderated when working with object COBOL.

Minimal knowledge of object technology is needed to create object wrappers for legacy COBOL programs. Software reuse is enhanced by rejuvenating literally hundreds, perhaps thousands, of older software modules through OO COBOL.

Frameworks represent another technique that can aid the practice of reuse. The concept of frameworks remains valid, although its association with the late, lamented Taligent enterprise has tarnished its image somewhat.

The overall benefit of frameworks is that they enable a higher level of code and design reuse than that which is practical with other design approaches. In addition to frameworks, there are certainly many other reuse technologies such as 4GLs, code generators, and class libraries. However, 4GLs and code generators are based on procedural programming techniques and cannot easily provide the infrastructure and design guidance that are possible with frameworks. While class libraries do improve code reuse, they provide functionality at a very low level and force the developer to provide the interconnections between the libraries.

Additionally, the benefits from frameworks and reuse are gained over time because the productivity gains do not come just from the first or second use, but from multiple uses of the technology. There are several benefits of using frameworks, but these summarize the major advantages:

- *Provides infrastructure and architectural guidance* – By virtue of the interconnections among the class libraries, much of the needed functionality already exists in the framework, thus reducing coding, testing, and debugging efforts. In addition, frameworks encourage better design in the code that developers write by providing an "example" to guide them to more effectively utilize object technology. Applications developed with frameworks tend to be smaller, and more maintainable and reusable.

- *Provides a mechanism for reliability extending functionality* – While objects and object classes provide interfaces for extending functionality at a fine-grained level, frameworks provide this flexibility at a higher level. In this way, applications can be developed by using the framework as a starting point and writing smaller amounts of code to modify or extend the framework's behavior. These extensions can be added without sacrificing compatibility and interoperability because the interfaces are well defined.

- *Reduces maintenance* – Due to inheritance, when a framework bug is fixed or a new feature is added, the benefits of those changes become available more quickly to the derived classes. Also, changes are made only in one place, thus, the chance of introducing additional errors in the code is minimized.

- *Greater reuse* – Abstraction and subclassing contribute to reuse of code. Frameworks, providing a subsystem design, contribute to reuse of design.

Improving developer productivity is a major challenge for the entire industry. While current approaches have advanced productivity, the next generation of software must fully exploit OOT to provide the productivity and development leverage that is needed to solve today's complex computing problems.

While the use of object technology has demonstrated the capability to increase developer productivity and enhance program maintainability, it is not just a matter of switching to OOT, but adopting how this technology is implemented. The success of OOT hinges on infrastructures similar to frameworks that enable developers to focus on the implementation of their functional expertise, design software that is more reusable and maintainable, and create innovative software that addresses business problems.

Frameworks and systems based on frameworks such as IBM's CommonPoint application system empower developers to approach the potential of improved design and code reuse, including reduced development requirements, reduced maintenance, and higher reliability. In addition, programming based on frameworks enables the developer to build a better integrated system.

## Standards

Standards already in the pipeline such as CORBA, OLE, and OpenDoc have been addressed earlier in this report. One of the more explosive products to have emerged in recent years, the OO language Java, may also enter the standards realm by the sheer weight of its popularity. Java has achieved de facto standard status, at least in the object technology sphere (see Figure 12.1).

## Figure 12.1 Java Development Diagram

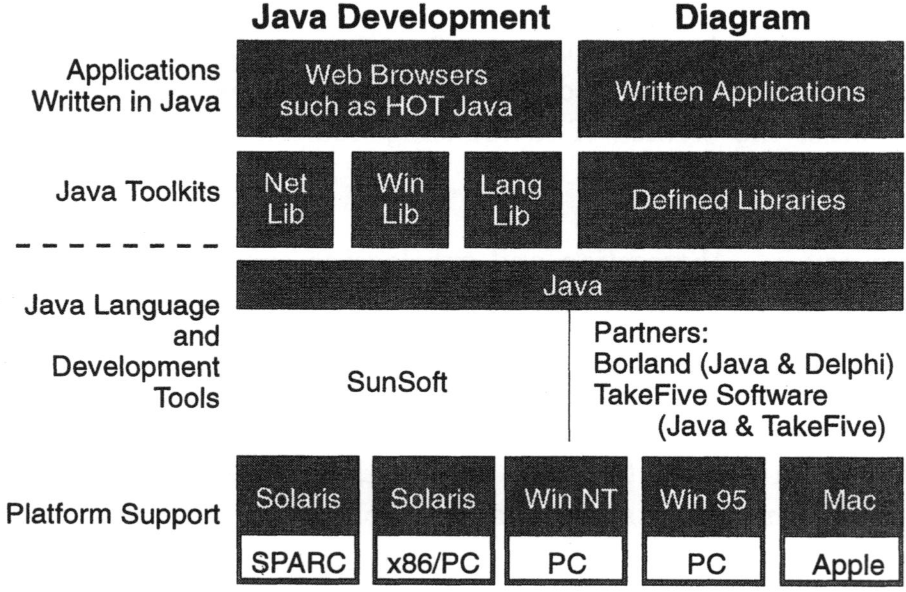


Java is easier to learn and program than C++, although it syntactically resembles the latter to a great degree. Java's association with Internet technology has further imbued it with an aura of high value that it might otherwise fail to possess.

Released by Sun Microsystems in 1995, Java's unique attributes were an immediate hit within the developer community. Some of its popular features include:

- Java-generated applications are portable

- Platform dependency has been reduced by compiling Java applications called applets into an intermediate language that is subsequently read by interpreters when executing on various Microsoft, Mac, and UNIX systems

- The language supports automatic memory management and dynamic binding, much in the mode of Smalltalk

- Cross-platform capabilities are further enhanced in Java through its precise definition of data types and arithmetic operators so as not to impede multiple system operations

Network support is particularly strong, an essential property with current distributed architectures. The Web's ubiquitous hypertext transfer protocol (HTTP), along with the Internet's widely used file transfer protocol (FTP), are among the protocols supported. A modicum of network security measures also have been added to Java's repertoire (see Figure 12.2).

## Figure 12.2 Java's Maximum Security Architecture

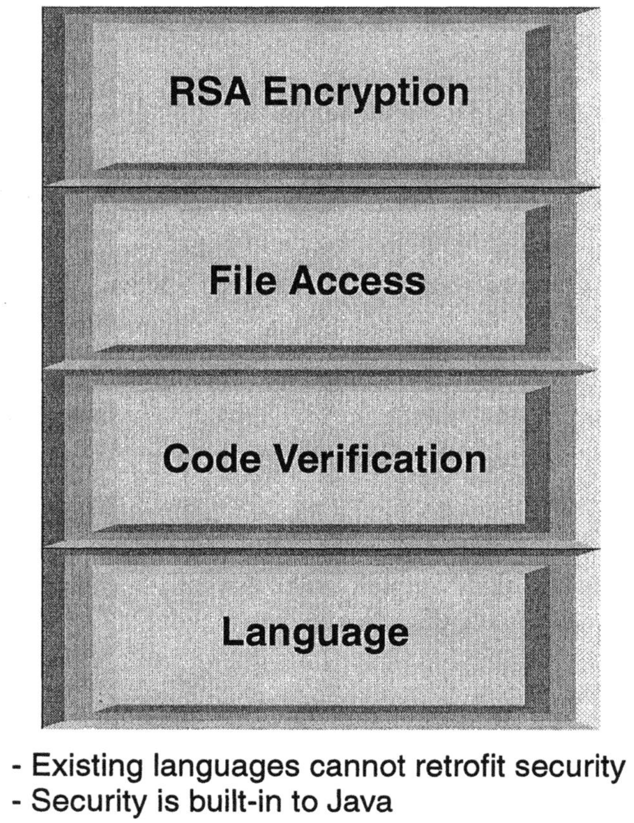

- Existing languages cannot retrofit security
- Security is built-in to Java

*Source: Sun*

One of the language's most popular attributes is the ability of Java applets to be integrated into the hypertext markup language (HTML) code of a Web page. Java-enabled browsers can download applets from a Web server for execution on a client vehicle. Because the language supports multithreaded processing, numerous applets can be instituted simultaneously.

Basically, Java brings multimedia support to Web pages, thus enhancing their appeal. This is a powerful factor for developers building Web sites for commercial purposes. Their ability to liven up the presentation through Java can determine the ultimate success or failure of a commercial Web page.

Any type of application can be invoked from a Web page in the Java environment, with subsequent operation possible on multiple platform types. The participating Web browser must be Java-compatible to achieve this.

Sun's HotJava browser was its first accomplice; Netscape's browser also offered early support; and virtually every major Web browser developer has followed suit.

Has Java attained de facto standard status? The answer has to be a resounding yes. Sun chose the correct option – it gave the technology away, rendering it a widespread phenomenon almost immediately. Sun also was incredibly lucky in the timing of Java's arrival. An absolute need was met by a relatively straightforward solution.

There are detractors, however. While Java's proponents boast about its inherent simplicity, a vocal minority decry its complexity. Proponents, of course, are comparing it to C++, whereas detractors relate it to HTML. HTML is not a full development language, and is thereby much easier to deploy than C++.

Sun's answer to the charge of Java's supposed complexity is JavaScript. As the title implies, JavaScript is a scripting language that can be used to modify the actions of Java applets. In other words, it is a development aid that can be used to fine-tune Java applications.

Java's primary focus to date has been on Internet development. It could just as easily become a vehicle for conventional application development. If the language achieves success in both worlds – general development and Web page generation – then Java may become almost a universal language in the world of technology. In practice, this will probably not happen as other vendors will not allow Sun to become the sole owner of a standard this powerful.

Microsoft for example, in its approach to Java, is wrapping applets in order that they may become an OLE object. This is a good strategy for Microsoft and its Windows environment. It does nothing for Java's portability, however. In fact, one might conclude Microsoft intends to pre-empt Java by endorsing it, adopting it, and indirectly controlling it through sheer marketing strength.

As Java further emerges from its early beginnings, practically all major software vendors are supporting its presence. The problem lies in the fact that each vendor is extending and customizing the language, thus harming its inherent cross-platform capabilities; a similar scenario to that is UNIX.

Despite these problems, Java will be a major force in application development for years to come. One reason is the lack of a comparable competitor. Language development is a thankless and often a profitless task. Not many vendors are rushing to build "the next Java." This alone guarantees it a successful future.

## OODBMS Products

Version 1.2 of the ODMG-93 standard was the initial release by the ODMG that focused on application portability among compliant OODBMS offerings. Included in these offerings was not just object databases, but tools, middleware, and associated software. This effort is comparable to SQL's mission in relational database environments.

Each of the two dozen or so members of the ODMG, most of whom are vendors, have made a commitment to harmonize their current and future OO product lines with the database standard. This will enable users to develop applications that are able to move from one OODBMS to another. Products can conform to the standard through several means: C++ and Smalltalk bindings, ODL, and OQL.

In a distributed environment, application portability may be vital. The main mechanism for achieving this portability is to impose standards, which is just what the ODMG specification and follow-on releases do for the industry.

One nagging problem with ODMG-93 activities has been a lack of participation by tools vendors. As shown in Table 12.1, there are few participants of that ilk. This may change over time, but tools will be essential to help users develop portable applications. Without tools it will be difficult to build OO applications.

## Table 12.1 ODMG-93 Loyalists

| Vendor | Product |
|---|---|
| ADB<br>Redwood Shores, California | Matisse (OODBMS) |
| Fujitsu Open Systems Solutions<br>San Jose, California | ODB II (object DBMS) |
| GemStone Systems<br>Beaverton, Oregon | GemStone (object DBMS) |
| Ibex Computing SA<br>Archemps, France | Itasca (object DBMS) |
| Micram Object Technology<br>Bochum, Germany | Micram (database creation tool) |
| Object Design<br>Burlington, Massachusetts | ObjectStore (object DBMS) |
| Objectivity<br>Mountain View, California | Objectivity/DB (object DBMS) |
| $O_2$ Technology<br>Palo Alto, California | The $O_2$ Systems (object DBMS) |
| Omniscience Object Technology<br>Santa Clara, California | Omniscience (object DBMS) |
| Ontos<br>Burlington, Massachusetts | Ontos DB (object DBMS) |
| Persistence Software<br>San Mateo, California | Poet (object DBMS) |
| Sybase<br>Emeryville, California | Sybase (RDBMS) |
| UniSQL<br>Austin, Texas | UniSQL (object/RDBMS) |
| Versant Object Technology<br>Menlo Park, California | Versant (object DBMS) |

# Distributed Object Management

Whether justified or not is debatable, but COM/OLE from Microsoft is the object technology in the lead today. This is true not just at the desktop development level, but it extends to the enterprise with recent additions targeted for distributed environments.

Perhaps the eventual scenario will find the desktop dominated by OLE, with CORBA ascendant on the backbone. If this happens, it is vital that linkage between the two entities be available, preferably in the guise of a standard.

OMG has labored long and hard on an approach whereby a user would be able to carry out an operation on a CORBA object from OLE-based applications. Private companies also have worked in this area. Among them are Iona Technologies, Expersoft, and Genesis Development.

At present, COM has seemingly more momentum as the OMG continues to wrestle with problems of portability and interoperability. COM, meanwhile, has the advantage of emanating from a homogeneous source (Microsoft), thus providing it with more control of its operating contingencies.

For distributed objects to achieve widespread support, security must be imposed. While not a critical element in research institutions and development laboratories, security gains in importance when leaving these environments.

For a distributed object system to be useful in the real world it must provide a means for secure access to objects and the data they encapsulate. The issues surrounding system object models are complex for corporate customers and software vendors making planning decisions in this area, but COM can be a solid foundation for an enterprisewide computing environment.

COM provides security along several dimensions. First, it uses standard OS permissions to determine whether a client (running in a particular user's security context) has the right to start the code associated with a particular class of object. Second, with respect to persistent objects (class code along with data stored in a persistent store such as file system or database), COM uses OS or application permissions to determine if a particular client can load the object at all, and if so whether they have read-only or read-write access. Finally, because its security architecture is based on the design of the DCE RPC security architecture, an industry-standard communications mechanism that includes fully authenticated sessions, COM provides cross-process and cross-network object servers with standard security information about the client or clients that are using it so a server can use security in a more sophisticated fashion than that of simple OS permissions or related techniques.

COM supports distributed objects; that is, it allows application developers to split a single application into a number of different component objects, each of which can run on a different computer. Because COM provides network transparency, these applications do not appear to be located on different machines. The entire network appears to be one large computer with enormous processing power and capacity.

Many single-process object models and programming languages exist today, and a few distributed object systems are available. However, few provide an identical, transparent programming model for small, in-process objects, medium out-of-process objects on the same machine, and potentially huge objects running on another machine on the network.

COM provides a transparent model, where a client uses an object in the same process in the same manner as it would use one on a machine many miles away. COM explicitly bars certain types of "features" – such as direct access to object data, properties or variables – that might be convenient in the case of in-process objects, but would make it impossible for an out-of-process object to provide the same set of services. This is called location transparency.

## OLE Directions

During the second half of the 1980s, the spread of workgroup and departmental computing environments brought increased attention to the need for sharing data and services across computing environments. At the same time, the evolution of open systems concepts propelled distributed computing issues to the forefront of standardization efforts, displacing portability as the primary openness strategy. Today, organizations with investments in heterogeneous hardware and software platforms are focusing on ways to achieve interoperability among applications, tools, and services as a means of integrating enterprise computing resources.

Although the desktop has been a major catalyst in the move toward distributed computing, today's emphasis is on standards for multiplatform, multivendor interoperability. This reflects the practical need in most organizations to exploit an existing base of heterogeneous systems and to preserve investments in those systems while migrating to an open environment.

Microsoft's strategy aims to extend the benefits of open systems to a wider range of users and computing environments by providing a consistent distributed computing solution for both proprietary and open environments. This, in turn, provides a bridge for organizations seeking to move from traditional, non-distributed systems to those that are both open and distributed.

Recognizing the need to respond to economic or competitive pressures ultimately forces an organization to seek new ways of addressing business realities. Often organizations have two choices, buy or build the solution. An organization can now buy, build or assemble the appropriate solution.

As the availability of OLE integration spreads across major enterprise platforms, the software industry will have achieved a component market that provides higher rates of innovation, more specialized customer solutions, better applications, and a faster, less expensive development process. Rather than building all components of a custom solution from scratch, corporate developers can purchase software components from specialized component vendors.

For instance, they might buy a financial analysis component or a customer information component for use in a custom application. In the process, users of the application get a higher quality product because the application incorporates the best components made by experts. Because corporate developers need not build each component from scratch, they can deliver the application in much less time and at a greatly reduced cost.

Further, components can be built and reused by in-house organizations. This will support the decentralization of development, and the separation of technical skills, business expertise, and skill level required to create an application.

In addition, business applications assembled using OLE component integration software are flexible. With modular software applications built using OLE, changing an application to meet new needs is easier because a new component from most vendors can be purchased and plugged into the application to extend its functionality. This process makes system maintenance easier and extends the life of the application.

In summary, OLE continues to be upgraded to meet the needs of the marketplace. Some of its new and planned features include:

- Improved spell checking

- Software accessibility for disabled persons

- Improved search and replace technique that supports full-flavored text formats

- Non-rectangular objects and regional windows

- Multiple level Undo procedure

- Multiple views per object, object flows, and layout negotiation among objects

# Appendix

---

## COBOL and Objects Do Mix

It may seem inconceivable to object purists, but, COBOL is now OO. It even supports inheritance, so it is a true OO product, not just "object-based."

Among the dozens of OO languages that have appeared on the scene, certainly C++ and Smalltalk are the most widely used. Well, COBOL will give them fierce competition, particularly in the business environments within which it functions best because the language's developers studied carefully the strengths and weaknesses of both C++ and Smalltalk.

The designers of OO COBOL stayed closer to the Smalltalk model than C++. This is evident in that everything is defined as an object, even integer values, much like the all-object Smalltalk approach. In this sense, OO COBOL is a "purer" object vehicle than is C++.

OO COBOL is similar to C++, however, in that both languages are hybrids. Programmers can create procedural routines along with objects according to the needs of the application. Unlike C++, OO COBOL offers backward compatibility with earlier versions of the language.

There have been four versions of ANSI-standard COBOL put forth over the years: COBOL 68, 74, 85, and the current 97 version. OO COBOL is a subset of the 97 version.

There are several products in the marketplace, each of which address more or less of the ANSI model. Hitachi's OO COBOL Version 2.x and IBM's

---

VisualAge for COBOL Version 1.x are representative of the products in this area (see Table A.1).

## Table A.1 COBOL Object Standards Compliance

| ANSI Feature | Hitachi OOC | Visual Age |
|---|:---:|:---:|
| Automatic garbage collection | ✓ | – |
| Classes | | |
| ◆ Class | ✓ | ✓ |
| ◆ Parameterized | – | – |
| ◆ Simple | – | – |
| Dynamic binding | ✓ | ✓ |
| Encapsulation | ✓ | ✓ |
| Inheritance | | |
| ◆ Single | ✓ | ✓ |
| ◆ Multiple | ✓ | ✓ |
| Interface construct | ✓ | – |
| Methods | | |
| ◆ Methods | ✓ | ✓ |
| ◆ Invariant | ✓ | – |
| ◆ Prototype | ✓ | – |
| Objects | | |
| ◆ Dynamic | ✓ | ✓ |
| ◆ Static | – | |
| ◆ Typed | ✓ | ✓ |
| ◆ Untyped | ✓ | ✓ |
| ◆ Factory | ✓ | – |
| ◆ Object modifiers | ✓ | – |
| ◆ Property of objects | ✓ | – |
| Repository | ✓ | ✓ |

Hitachi offers a compiler that comes close to matching COBOL 97 specifications. IBM has leveraged the features of its SOM object technology while also adhering to many COBOL 97 mandates.

Perhaps the strongest attribute of Hitachi's OO COBOL is its adherence to the ANSI standard, along with excellent debugging capabilities (its diagnostics are very precise). It does, however, require that Identification, Data, and Procedure Division headers be declared for each method in an object. This step generates a lot of clutter in the coding structure.

VisualAge for COBOL, as the name implies, provides an excellent visual programming environment. IBM's compiler also supports program development with a robust set of tools. These include a graphical debugger, a GUI builder, an application analyzer, as well as the compiler itself. IBM's shortcoming, if any, is in its lesser support for the ANSI specification.

The emergence of OO COBOL provides another entry in the object technology sweepstakes. Considering the vast reservoir of COBOL-based applications now active in the marketplace, OO COBOL should breathe new life to programmers who have been, up to now, stranded in a technological stifled by nonforward-thinking product developers.

www.ingramcontent.com/pod-product-compliance
Ingram Content Group UK Ltd.
Pitfield, Milton Keynes, MK11 3LW, UK
UKHW050840080726
13597UKWH00035B/176